Civic Solitude

Civic Solitude

Why Democracy Needs Distance

ROBERT B. TALISSE

OXFORD
UNIVERSITY PRESS

Oxford University Press is a department of the University of Oxford.
It furthers the University's objective of excellence in research, scholarship,
and education by publishing worldwide. Oxford is a registered trade mark of
Oxford University Press in the UK and in certain other countries.

Published in the United States of America by Oxford University Press
198 Madison Avenue, New York, NY 10016, United States of America.

© Oxford University Press 2024

All rights reserved. No part of this publication may be reproduced, stored in a retrieval system, transmitted, used for text and data mining, or used for training artificial intelligence, in any form or by any means, without the prior permission in writing of Oxford University Press, or as expressly permitted by law, by license or under terms agreed with the appropriate reprographics rights organization. Inquiries concerning reproduction outside the scope of the above should be sent to the Rights Department, Oxford University Press, at the address above.

You must not circulate this work in any other form
and you must impose this same condition on any acquirer

CIP data is on file at the Library of Congress

ISBN 9780197752166

DOI: 10.1093/9780197752197.001.0001

Printed by Integrated Books International, United States of America

Contents

Preface		vii
Acknowledgments		xiii

1. Setting the Stage — 1
   1.1 Clarifying the Thesis — 4
   1.2 The Character of the Argument — 9
   1.3 The Curative Fallacy — 11
   1.4 Democratic Theory and Democratic Politics — 16
   1.5 Sketching the Argument — 20
   1.6 Starting Small — 27

2. What Does Democracy Look Like? — 29
   2.1 Looking for Democracy — 29
       2.1.1 Democracy in the Streets — 29
       2.1.2 Democracy in the Voting Booth — 35
   2.2 Democracy as a Social Ideal — 37
       2.2.1 *Can We Live Together as Equals?* — 38
       2.2.2 Equal Standing — 41
       2.2.3 Coercion without Subordination — 43
   2.3 What Citizens Owe to One Another — 45
       2.3.1 Public-Mindedness — 47
       2.3.2 Responsiveness and Transparency — 49
       2.3.3 Civility — 54
           2.3.3.1 Civility as a Norm of Recognition — 54
           2.3.3.2 Civility and the Imagination — 56
           2.3.3.3 Civility and the Uncivil — 57
   2.4 Does Democracy Exist? — 59
   2.5 What Democracy Looks Like — 63

3. Our Polarization Problem — 65
   3.1 Getting Our Bearings — 68
   3.2 Two Kinds of Polarization — 70
       3.2.1 Political Polarization — 70

			3.2.1.1 Three Sites of Political Polarization	71
			3.2.1.2 The Three Sites as Mutually Reinforcing	75
		3.2.2	Belief Polarization	77
			3.2.2.1 How Belief Polarization Works	81
			3.2.2.2 Belief Polarization and the Stadium	85
		3.2.3	A Review	87
	3.3	Centering the Partisan Self: Sorting and Saturation		89
	3.4	The Polarization Dynamic		95
		3.4.1	How the Dynamic Works	95
		3.4.2	The Real Problem of Polarization	99
	3.5	Democracy's Autoimmune Disorder		103
4.	The Need for Solitude			106
	4.1	Expanding Civic Responsibility		109
	4.2	Managing Polarization		116
		4.2.1	The Relational Approach: Facilitated Democracy	116
			4.2.1.1 Aristotelian Underpinnings	117
			4.2.1.2 Assessing the Program	119
		4.2.2	Decentering the Partisan Self	124
			4.2.2.1 The Personal Approach	125
			4.2.2.2 Decentering Explained	130
	4.3	Politics Alone		134
		4.3.1	Two Kinds of Distance	135
		4.3.2	The Practice of Atopia	138
			4.3.2.1 "Was Aristotle a Conservative?"	139
			4.3.2.2 The Value of Atopia	141
		4.3.3	Spaces of Solitude	145
		4.3.4	Is Civic Solitude Elitist?	148
	4.4	Conclusion		152
Epilogue: Democracy—The Task Within Us				154
Notes				163
Works Cited				171
Index				183

Preface

I had no idea I was writing the first book in a trilogy when I began working on *Overdoing Democracy* (2019). I took myself instead to be producing a focused monograph devoted to a relatively narrow point. Specifically, I was arguing that the goods of democracy can thrive only in the presence of other, nonpolitical social goods. This means that when democracy takes over our lives, it undermines itself. I concluded that if democracy is to flourish, we must reclaim aspects of social life for nonpolitical cooperative activities. At the time, this seemed an uncontroversial idea that had been overlooked in current democratic theory and needed to be expressed. To my surprise, though, *Overdoing Democracy* struck a nerve. In the course of talking about the book with both academic and popular audiences, I realized that I needed to push the argument further. The claim that we need sometimes to do nonpolitical things together presses the question of how we should proceed when it is, indeed, time for politics.

This prompted a second book, *Sustaining Democracy* (2021). There, I argued that citizens must uphold democratic relations with their partisan opponents, even though they often have compelling moral reasons to suspend them. My argument drew on a range of empirical considerations suggesting that in the absence of civil relations with opponents, we lose the capacity to maintain democratically healthy coalitions with our allies. We must sustain democracy with our political foes if we are to sustain democracy with our political friends.

The trouble is that our social lives are saturated with the escalated tensions and animosities of partisanship; thus, we *already* hold our political rivals in contempt. How, then, can we restore civil relations with those who we have written off as unfit for democracy?

Sustaining Democracy concluded with a tentative proposal regarding how we might be able to sustain democracy with those whose politics we despise. I proposed that we must find ways to engage with our opposition *at a distance* from them. We must encounter their objections to our views in settings that do not involve the kind of face-to-face confrontation that is likely only to provoke our latent hostilities for the other side. *Sustaining Democracy* closed with the thought that citizens need sometimes to engage in a mode of political thinking that is secluded from political allies and adversaries alike.

Civic Solitude completes the trilogy by developing that theme. My central contention here is that responsible democratic citizenship calls for occasions where one can engage in solitary reflection on civic matters that transcend the rivalries of the political present. Civic solitude thus involves an exercise of the imagination; it calls for contemplation of political conditions that are not already packaged in the idiom of the toxic partisan fissures of contemporary democracy. Crucially, the aim of this practice is not to take leave of the political fray, but rather to dislodge the partisan tendencies that cause our political engagements to be democratically deficient, because they are rooted in cognitive and affective dynamics that erode our capacity to treat our fellow citizens as our equals. Solitary civic reflection of the proposed kind is thus an act of democratic citizenship, not a withdrawal from it.

From this sketch, we can see that the trilogy is focused on the *ethics of citizenship*, the moral responsibilities and challenges that fall to us as members of a democratic society. Although each work in the trilogy is addressed to a distinct topic, they reflect a common diagnostic idea: There are ways in which democracy can unravel even when—indeed, *because*—citizens are striving in earnest to fulfill their civic responsibilities. That is, some political dysfunctions are *internal* to democracy. They reside within the democratic ideal;

they arise out of democracy's practices. The trilogy is devoted to the idea that democracy is subject to something like an autoimmune disorder.

I realize how odd that sounds, so allow me to elaborate. John Dewey and Jane Addams are both credited with the principle that "the cure for democracy's ills is more democracy." Their idea is that all political problems owe to a *deficit* in democracy, our *falling short* of what democracy requires. From this, it's natural to assert that *more* democracy—by which they mean *better* democracy—is always the correct prescription for any problem democracy might face.

The allure of the Dewey-Addams principle is undeniable. Indeed, much of what is awry with our politics is due to our institutions, practices, and attitudes being insufficiently democratic. Dewey and Addams are to this extent correct. More democracy surely is the correct response to those problems.

Yet we must resist the conclusion that more democracy is *always* the proper response to democracy's ills. The Dewey-Addams principle assumes that the values, priorities, and responsibilities of democracy form an internally consistent set, that the pursuit of one component of the democratic ideal can never involve the endangering of another. One theme underlying this trio of books is that this assumption is false. Certain capacities that are necessary for responsible citizenship can be eroded in the course of indispensable forms of democratic participation. While satisfying one dimension of our civic duty, we can jeopardize our capacity to meet other democratic responsibilities. It follows that the Dewey-Addams principle is wrong. Not *every* difficulty that democracy confronts is due to a democratic deficit. More democracy cannot be the prescription for ills that are internal to democracy itself.

Acknowledging the internal nature of some of democracy's troubles complicates our thinking about how democracy can be repaired. Put simply, if some of democracy's difficulties arise from our striving in earnest to meet our civic responsibilities, those difficulties cannot be eliminated from democracy, but only *mitigated*. Mitigation strategies are not elixirs, but ways of managing obstacles that cannot be eradicated. This helps to explain why, despite the fact that they are focused on the same dysfunctions, the three books make distinct proposals. In a nutshell, *Overdoing Democracy* argues that we must sometimes do nonpolitical things with others; *Sustaining Democracy* makes the case that we need to sustain civil relations even with our political foes; and this book argues that we must sometimes do politics all by ourselves. Throughout these works, my claim has been that the proposed mitigations are at best partial—things we need to do *in addition to* the other steps we must take in order to uphold democracy.

On almost any account, democracy is a demanding political proposal. The view I develop in this trilogy reveals that it might be more demanding than is usually supposed, as it entails that democracy is *intrinsically* burdened by conflicts that reside within the office of citizenship. As there is no fix for democracy's internal difficulties, there is no end to them either. Thus, democracy is never fully established but must be continually sustained. As John Dewey correctly noted in a different context, democracy is an ongoing project, always a "task before us." Building on the preceding two works, this book argues that the democratic task before us is partly a task *within* each of us.

Although this book completes a trilogy, it is written to be a standalone work. No familiarity with *Overdoing Democracy* or *Sustaining Democracy* has been presumed. Consequently, those who *are* familiar with the previous two books are bound to find some thematic repetition. This is of course unavoidable, but I assure the reader that there is no outright *replication* of material presented in the earlier books. I have endeavored to come at these topics anew, and even at junctures where I revisit points I have made previously, I believe I have added something novel that reflects an improvement in my thinking. Whether I have succeeded in this last respect is for the reader to determine, of course.

This book is like its companions in being an academic book written for a general readership. Among other things, this means that I have tried to write in straightforward and accessible prose, eliminating as far as possible the jargon and other devices of academic political philosophy. Scholarly citations hence have been limited only to what is strictly necessary. As a result, the book contains minimal discussion of the major works and figures in the history of democratic theory. Readers who wish to follow up on the empirical research I discuss will find the appropriate references and commentary in the notes, while those who seek simply to attend to my central argument may disregard the notes entirely. In short, I have attempted to write a philosophically astute book about democracy that can be read by my fellow citizens.

Given my intended audience, I concentrate mainly on the specific context of the United States. This is the democracy I'm most familiar with. But it also happens to be a democracy where the particular internal pathologies with which I am concerned are both prevalent and well documented. I will argue in the coming chapters that these dysfunctions—roughly, unsustainable levels of polarization, partisan animosity, and in-group homogeneity—are products of certain tendencies within the social psychology of human beings; therefore, although the account is focused on the United States, the difficulties I identify ought not be dismissed as *unique* or *peculiar* to the United States. To be clear, other contemporary democracies are not beset by these dysfunctions to the exaggerated degree that one finds in the United States. But none are entirely free of them, either. I think that in this regard, the United States usefully serves as a bellwether, or at least a warning about some of the troubles that can emerge in pursuit of the democratic ideal.

I am completing work on this book in the early stages of a potentially pivotal presidential election season in my country. As I write, the leading presidential candidate for one of the major parties is facing several indictments relating to attempts to obstruct the transfer of power after he lost the 2020 presidential election. Meanwhile, the incumbent president faces low approval, even among likely voters within his party. It seems odd, then, to be completing a book about the need for citizens to occasionally step away from the public and collective facets of democracy and engage in solitary political reflection. Too much is at stake, one might claim.

Although this book isn't exactly optimistic, it nonetheless embraces the hope that we haven't reached the end of the line for democracy in the United States. Despite all of the urgency and angst of our political present, we must not lose sight of the fact that democracy is an ongoing project of maintenance, repair, and renovation. Democracy always looks ahead. A good deal of democratic theory and practice accepts this point, and yet sees the democratic project as focused on the external architecture and machinery of democracy. According to these views, democracy calls us to look to the next election, the upcoming legislative decision, or the next opportunity for institutional reform. Indeed, that *is* central to the democratic endeavor. Democracy thrives on forward-looking collective action. Yet this book demonstrates that democracy also sets a *personal* task for each of us, individually. If democracy is to succeed, we must sustain our civic dispositions. To this extent, looking ahead is also looking within.

Acknowledgments

This work is about the value of solitude, but one never really writes a book alone. Throughout the process of writing these pages, I benefitted enormously from friends and colleagues. Some read draft chapters and offered generous comments; others tolerated me asking questions and discussing the manuscript; and then there were those who provided other forms crucial support, I suspect often without even realizing it. In any case, I thank the following people for their assistance: Scott Aikin, Elizabeth Anderson, Theano Apostolou, Jody Azzouni, Heather Battaly, Joseph Biehl, Oliver Burkeman, Steven Cahn, Michael Calamari, Gregg Caruso, Allan Carey, Myisha Cherry, Edward Clark, Matthew Congdon, Matthew Cotter, Derrick Darby, Lisa Disch, Elizabeth Edenberg, Kevin Elliott, Zachary Elwood, David Estlund, Carrie Figdor, Sanford Goldberg, Lenn Goodman, Alex Guerrero, Jun Han, Michael Hannon, Michael Harbour, Nicole Heller, Diana Heney, Marc Hetherington, David Hildebrand, Michael Hodges, David Hoinski, Shanto Iyengar, Magdi Jacobs, David Kaspar, Daniel A. Kaufman, Ben Klutsey, Chandran Kukathas, John Lachs, Helene Landemore, Lawrence Lessig, Katherine Loevy, Holly Longair, Alyssa Lowery, Mason Marshall, Takunda Matose, David McCullough, Amy McKiernan, Christian Miller, Joshua Miller, Cheryl Misak, Ryan Muldoon, Karen Ng, Jon Olfasson, John Palomino, Fabienne Peter, John Peterman, Lyn Radke, Yvonne Raley, Jonathan Rauch, Regina Rini, Melvin Rogers, Wendy Salkin, Timothy J. Shaffer, Seana Shiffrin, Peter Simpson, Scott Stroud, Paul Taylor, Jeffrey Tlumak, Robert Tempio, Piers Turner, Rebecca Tuvel, Sarah Tyson, Kevin Vallier, Isaac Wagner, Brandon Warmke, Leif Wenar, and Julian Wuerth.

I also thank audiences at Stanford University, University College London, University of Copenhagen, University of St. Andrews, University of Cincinnati, Bowling Green State University, Chapman University, University of Texas at Austin, Corning Community College, University of Iceland, Tulane University, University of Nevada at Reno, Pacific University, Pepperdine University, University of Colorado at Denver, Rollins College, Northeastern University, University of Massachusetts at Boston, Syracuse University, Fordham Law School, West Virginia University, Vanderbilt University, The Jewish Theological Seminary, The Heterodox Academy, The Global Forum on Modern Direct Democracy (Lucerne, Switzerland), and The Institute of Philosophy (London).

I also benefitted greatly from the support of The Institute for Humane Studies, which provided a grant that enabled me to organize a workshop at Vanderbilt on the penultimate draft of the manuscript. I thank the participants in that workshop—William James Booth, Ismail Kurun, Michael Lynch, Eduardo Martinez, Julia Maskivker, and Dana Nelson—for feedback and criticism that vastly improved the book.

I owe a special expression of gratitude to Lucy Randall, my editor at Oxford University Press, for her excellent judgment and ongoing enthusiasm for my work.

On a more personal note, my largest debt is to Joanne Billett, whose distinctive brand of encouragement enables me to explore the world of ideas without losing contact with the ground.

1
Setting the Stage

"This is what democracy looks like." A Google Image search for that phrase instantly delivers thousands of photos depicting the same thing: masses of people assembled in a public space, acting together to express a shared political sentiment. Judging from these pictures, democracy has a distinctive appearance. It looks like people engaging in public collective action.

This makes good sense. Democracy is rule by the people. In a democracy, the people are equal partners in collective self-government, co-authors of the political order they inhabit together. They are *citizens* rather than *subjects*. For this reason, they are not mere spectators. Democratic citizens are full participants in politics.

Of course, in contemporary large-scale societies, citizens rule themselves indirectly. Democracy is facilitated by a range of characteristic institutions and processes, including periodic elections that fill public offices. Modern democracy thus is *representative* democracy. The people elect officials, and the officials represent the people's interests and priorities.

Even though elections loom large in democracy, citizenship is not confined to the voting booth. Without a vigilant citizenry, democracy dissolves into rule by elites, and often something worse. After the votes are cast and decisions are enacted, citizens still must *evaluate* their government and, when necessary, hold representatives to account. In order to rule themselves, then, the people must make their voices heard beyond election day. They must take responsibility for the political order they collectively author. Public assembly and other modes of political action are thus essential to self-government.

This explains the search results. Any picture of democracy should focus on citizens engaged in their distinctive civic role. It should show them enacting self-government. It is no surprise, then, that the images depict democracy as something that happens "in the streets," when citizens take ownership of their politics.

I find this inspiring. As I see it, democracy is the contention that a decent political order is possible in the absence of royals, masters, and lords. It claims that people can maintain a free society all on their own. Democracy is thus a dignifying proposal. The Google images capture that dignity.

Yet this book advances a thesis that may seem incompatible with the enthusiasm I have just professed. I will argue that a certain kind of solitude is necessary for good citizenship. Maybe democracy isn't found in the streets after all.

When stated so bluntly, my thesis sounds implausible. This is because our thinking about citizenship tends to focus exclusively on democracy's collective and public aspects. We typically see citizenship as something that is practiced out in the open, where everyone can see. As a result, we regard solitude as a fundamentally non-civic condition, a flight from democracy. Solitude is hence regarded as paradigmatically *nonpolitical*. How, then, could it be an element of good democratic citizenship?

The seeming implausibility of my thesis deepens with the observation that solitude is commonly treated as a condition of privilege. When we think of solitude, our minds gravitate to images of affluent people relaxing in comfort, oblivious to the world around them. We link solitude to privacy, privacy to leisure, and leisure to luxury. Solitude thus is coupled with social advantage and political complacency. It might be thought that given the troubled state of our democracy, complacency is the last thing we need from citizens. Once again the claim that solitude is necessary for good citizenship seems a nonstarter.

Given the strength of these associations, my thesis must be unpacked with care. The entire book attempts to do this. After examining troubling dysfunctions that have beset our democracy, I will suggest that a particular kind of solitary reflective activity—what I call *civic solitude*—is a necessary element of any viable response. To put things simply, I will argue that democratic citizens need occasionally to occupy spaces where they can be alone with their thoughts, places where they can engage in a kind of civic reflection that is detached from the fray of partisan political struggles. Democracy happens when citizens collectively take to the streets, but a distinctive act of democratic citizenship can occur when individuals step into a public library, park, or museum.

Of course, this proposal is offered as a conjecture. The civic value of solitude has not been duly investigated by democratic theorists and practitioners. Many of my claims about the need for solitude await empirical confirmation. My aim, then, is modest. I hope to develop the idea of civic solitude in a way that makes it seem worth exploring. The intended upshot is that civic solitude is something we should try.

The speculative nature of the proposal does not mean that my overall position comes to nothing more than advice-giving. The case for civic solitude rests on a decisive argument about the nature of democratic citizenship. Specifically, I will reject the idea that all civic activity is public and collective. Although democracy is most recognizable "in the streets," responsible citizenship demands more than our participation in public political action. Accordingly, whatever you might think of the proposal for civic solitude, the coming argument should convince you that there's more to democratic citizenship than meets the eye.

Yet the idea that the civic is necessarily public and collective is firmly embedded in our political thinking. Dislodging it calls for an elaborate argument that engages core issues in political philosophy while making use of empirical findings in political psychology. Combining these two fields of inquiry into a single view of citizenship presents distinctive challenges. It may be helpful, then, to start with the big picture. The hope is that by bringing the background into focus, the coming details will more easily fall into place. This chapter sets the stage.

1.1 Clarifying the Thesis

The first task is to clarify the book's thesis. To do this, we need to step back. I noted earlier that the thesis that citizens need solitude may seem to undercut my professed enthusiasm for democracy. Yet some readers might associate my thesis with a more hostile stance. Civic solitude is a kind of solitude, after all. In calling for solitude, it may seem as if I am proposing that citizens should be politically apathetic and more inclined to leave politics to others—officials, elites, experts, and so on. Some will suspect that I am promoting a skeptical stance toward democracy.

This suspicion is understandable, even if misplaced. The rise of authoritarian movements within contemporary democracies has led many to conclude that ordinary people are too ignorant, irrational, or corruptible to uphold democracy. Accordingly, several recent books have defended various forms of skepticism about democracy.[1]

This book is not of that ilk. Yes, the coming chapters will examine dysfunctions that have beset contemporary democracy. And, moreover, I will argue that those dysfunctions are *internal* to democracy and thus cannot be eliminated. But I am no democracy skeptic. The thesis that democratic citizens need a kind of solitude is a claim about the requirements of citizenship, after all. The book is committed to improving democracy, rather than diluting or abandoning it.

Even setting democratic skepticism aside, the idea that solitude is necessary for responsible citizenship may still sound unpromising. According to a range of indicators, citizens today are confronting an epidemic of alienation, even loneliness.[2] Feelings of detachment and isolation arguably are at the root of many of our social problems. It seems plausible to think that we need to revitalize social connections and forge deeper community. How can solitude help?

Again, the book as a whole presents the case for the civic value of solitude. But the above concern can be addressed by noting, first, that it's not simple *aloneness* that I will contend is politically important. I will not be arguing that citizens need to take a hike on a deserted trail, retreat to a cabin on Walden Pond, or practice mindfulness. Although the argument will be that citizens need settings where they can gain distance from others, my claim is not that democratic citizens need solitude *as such*. My thesis is not that citizens need *simple* solitude, but *civic* solitude. The idea is that solitude provides the appropriate setting for a mode of political reflection that is essential for responsible citizenship. If this is correct, there is a kind of civic activity that can be engaged only in solitude. Hence the book's title.

Similarly, this book is not about respite from politics. My claim is not that citizens need occasionally to step away from democracy. To be sure, citizens might benefit from intervals of withdrawal. Intermittent departures from politics could be necessary for avoiding burnout. My 2019 book *Overdoing Democracy* advanced a version of this idea.[3] But that assertion is not at issue here. Instead, I am claiming there is a *civic activity* that calls for solitude. Solitude is needed for responsible democratic citizenship, then, not because we need political vacations, but rather because solitude provides the setting within which a certain fundamental democratic activity can be engaged. Civic solitude is not political downtime.

This book also is not a romantic celebration of the self-reliant individual. It does not indict common people as mediocre herd animals dedicated to suppressing singular geniuses. The claim is not that we need to find ways of detaching wholly from society so that we might realize our true freedom. I am concerned with what we owe to our fellow citizens. I will argue that in order to meet the demands of responsible citizenship, we need occasions for solitude. Satisfying those demands helps to sustain community with others. Civic solitude hence aims to *restore* democratic relations.

Finally, I am not claiming that solitary civic activity is *sufficient* for responsible citizenship. I am not proposing civic solitude as citizenship's only requirement. My view is that democratic citizens need occasions for solitude. But that's not *all* they need. In other words, civic solitude is not meant to *displace* more familiar forms of democratic collective action of the kind represented in the Google search. Civic solitude is an *additional* site of responsibility, a separate mode of political engagement that, I shall argue, is essential to good citizenship.

This last point calls for elaboration, even at this preliminary stage. In Chapter 2, I will develop the view that democracy is the aspiration to realize a self-governing society of political equals. One upshot of this aspiration is that citizens must participate in various political processes, many of which require them to act together in public. For example, they must sometimes build coalitions, share information, get involved, speak out, act in concert, and so on. Democratic theorists differ on the stringency of these requirements, of course. But there's no denying that citizens have a general duty to engage together in various forms of public action. These activities are necessary because they help to keep democratic government responsive to the people.

But there's more to democracy than that. Collective political activity is only one dimension of responsible citizenship. Insofar as democracy is the aspiration to realize a society of *equals*, citizens also have responsibilities to one another. Specifically, they must recognize one another's equal political standing. They must not treat their fellow citizens as inferiors, subordinates, pawns, or mere obstacles. This means that each citizen's political activism must be directed by consideration of their fellow citizens' perspectives, values, and priorities. Citizens hence have a duty to consult with their fellow citizens, including those with whom they disagree.

In contemporary societies, the required consultation is of necessity indirect. There simply isn't the time, space, or cognitive bandwidth for each citizen to engage with every other. Some of the familiar institutions of democracy lighten the load. Parties, interest groups, representative offices, and a free Press enable citizens to discern others' perspectives. But institutions go only so far. Even when they are effective, citizens must also *imagine* their way into the outlooks of their fellow citizens; they must endeavor to see things from *their* points of view. All of this means that citizens must be *reflective*. Responsible citizenship is partly a matter of engaging in certain kinds of thinking. Democracy happens in the streets, but it also goes on *inside* of us.

Thus far, we arrived at the platitude that citizens need to be both active and reflective. Now here's the rub: a range of empirical findings suggest that essential modes of collective action tend to corrode the reflective capacities that citizens need if they are to regard others as their political equals. These findings are taken up in Chapter 3, where I introduce *the polarization dynamic*, a collection of mutually reinforcing cognitive, affective, and social tendencies that are activated in collective democratic action, but which dismantle capacities for democratic reflection.

At the core of this dynamic is the phenomenon of *belief polarization*: when likeminded people interact mainly with one another, they become more extreme in their beliefs and dispositions. In the context of politics, belief polarization means that as we engage with our allies, we become more strident advocates of our political ideas. As this happens, conformity within our coalition mounts, while animosity for perceived outsiders intensifies. And as our networks become more homogeneous and more hostile toward outsiders, belief polarization accelerates. In turn, partisan animosity and in-group homogeneity escalate. This incentivizes political agents of various kinds—officeholders, candidates, party leaders, and so on—to amplify their partisan unity and cross-party antagonism. This then loops back to the citizens. Thus the polarization *dynamic*.

Once the details are in place, we will see that the polarization dynamic erodes our ability to treat our fellow citizens as our political equals. The crucial additional point is that we are *already* immersed in social environments that activate these processes. This suggests that we cannot restore these capacities by engaging in more, or even better, collective public action.

A more subtle formulation of my thesis is now in view. Certain reflective capacities that are necessary for responsible citizenship are eroded by democratically indispensable forms of public political activity. Specifically, capacities for imagination and perspective-taking are essential to regarding our fellow citizens as our equals, but they can be smothered in the course of democratic collective action. Thus, our fundamental conjecture: in order to cultivate and restore those capacities, we occasionally need distance from the fray of politics so that we can engage in a distinctive kind of civic contemplation. In this way, solitude is necessary for responsible democratic citizenship because it provides the setting for an essential civic activity.

Details regarding this mode of contemplation will come in Chapter 4. For now, note that the claim that citizens need solitude is compatible with a full-bodied endorsement of democratic activism. The idea is not that citizens need solitary reflection *instead* of political participation; rather, it is that acts of solitary reflection are necessary for preserving the democratic character of our collective political activities. Democracy may look like people engaged in collective political action, but there's more to democracy than can be captured in a photograph. To repeat, responsible citizenship is a matter of what goes on within us, too.

I hope that the foregoing remarks have clarified my thesis. I realize that I have yet to present an argument for thinking it true. No doubt, the discussion thus far has given rise to many questions.

Before proceeding, though, a few additional preliminaries must be addressed.

1.2 The Character of the Argument

To better situate the coming argument, it will help to say something about the *kind* of argument it is. This is a work in normative democratic theory. Here's what that means. When thinking about politics, it is common to distinguish *normative* views from *descriptive* views. To put matters very roughly, views of the former kind are concerned with what *ought* to be, while those in the latter category aim only to capture what is. By characterizing this book as a work in *normative* democratic theory, then, I indicate that it proposes a view about what ought to be—or, more precisely, how things should be in a democracy. Specifically, I will develop a normative view of democratic citizenship. I do not seek merely to describe how democratic citizens behave. Rather, I am proposing a view about the kind of citizens we ought to be—or strive to be.

Yet this is not a book about utopia. I do not aim to identify the responsibilities of citizens living in a perfect world. The normative account I will develop is rooted in the society we inhabit. I present a view of our responsibilities as citizens *given* current challenges confronting democracy. As I noted earlier, citizens of modern democracies live under conditions that initiate the polarization dynamic. The book presents a conception of our civic responsibilities in light of that fact. The normative position hence is based on a description of certain dysfunctions of citizenship. In this way, the proposed account will combine normative and empirical considerations.

This introduces a further characteristic of the argument. This book engages in a *particular style* of normative theorizing about democracy. To explain, some normative theories simply identify how things ought to be, but do not recommend a course of action. By contrast, this work is *prescriptive*. It is focused on what we ought to *do*. I prescribe a practice that citizens ought to adopt in response to the polarization dynamic.

Next consider the nature of the prescription. As I mentioned earlier, I will be focused on dysfunctions that are the *internal* to democracy. That is, I will argue that responsible forms of democratic political action heighten our exposure to the polarization dynamic. Consequently, the tendencies toward that dynamic cannot be eradicated from our democratic practices. The prescription for civic solitude thus is not offered as a *cure* for the polarization dynamic, but rather as a *mitigation*. The practice of civic solitude aims to counteract the polarization dynamic. We can say, then, that the prescription developed in this book is of a particular sort. It is a prescription for *remediation*. Accordingly, we can say that this is a work of *remedial* democratic theory.

Emphasizing the remedial nature of the account helps to underline its restricted scope. For one thing, my argument focuses on defects that plague particular contemporary democracies. For reasons that were mentioned in the Preface, I will be concentrating on the United States. The analysis thus is anchored mainly to that political context. To be sure, many of the dysfunctions of democracy in the United States can be found in other modern democratic societies; but these broader connections will not be explored here. My argument is that, *given* the prevalence of the polarization dynamic in the United States, citizens of that democracy need to create occasions for civic solitude. Consequently, even though I believe that civic solitude is a component of responsible citizenship across the board, the argument is not addressed to all democracies, but only those, like the United States, that are in the grip of the polarization dynamic.

But this restriction should not be overstated. There is reason to think that when it comes to the polarization dynamic, the United States serves as a bellwether. Moreover, as I mentioned, the dynamic emerges from deep-seated tendencies within human psychology. It represents a vulnerability of democracy as such, and should not be dismissed as exclusive to the United States. Those lucky enough to live in democracies that are not significantly afflicted by the polarization dynamic should take my argument as a warning about problematic tendencies that beset their pursuit of the democratic ideal.

The remedial prescription is restricted in two additional ways that warrant notice. First, civic solitude is not a panacea. It is not proposed as a remedy for all of democracy's ills. Other kinds of democratic deficiencies will no doubt call for different measures. For example, civic solitude is not offered as a fitting response to the forms of corruption that money has brought to our politics or the injustice of mass incarceration. Rather, my expectation is that civic solitude provides one part of a more comprehensive strategy for democratic restoration in response to the full range of dysfunctions contemporary democracy presently confronts. Second, civic solitude is also not proposed as *sufficient* for addressing the polarization dynamic. My contention instead is that it is *necessary* for remediating that dysfunction. A complete program for correcting democracy in light of the polarization dynamic will include various other interventions. In this way, civic solitude is not a *rival* to other prescriptions for recovering democracy. It complements them.

1.3 The Curative Fallacy

The next bit of stage-setting involves a slight detour. I hope it will not exhaust the reader's patience. We must address the fact that remedial theorizing invites a suspicious pattern of reasoning. Flagging that pattern can help us to avoid it.

Let's start with the pattern. In thinking about what to do in response to a problem, we intuitively try to locate its cause. Indeed, identifying the cause of a difficulty is often a necessary step in better understanding what it is. Once the cause is located, it then can seem natural to infer that the problem can be rectified by removing its cause. We seek to treat the problem rather than manage its symptoms. This, we tend to think, calls for the elimination of its underlying source. Reasonably, we thus prescribe measures that eradicate the cause of the problem.

This is an attractive mode of prescriptive reasoning, and in many contexts, it is reliable. For instance, imagine someone who is experiencing unusually intense fatigue. A physician conducts a blood test and discovers an abnormally low level of iron in the person's blood, but no other irregularities. Realizing that iron deficiency can cause fatigue, the physician prescribes an iron supplement. The fatigue subsides. Or take a patient experiencing high blood pressure. Reviewing the patient's diet, a physician prescribes a significant reduction in sodium intake. Blood pressure normalizes. In both cases, the ailment is treated by removing its cause.

But not all problems are like this. Recall the corny old joke: *The horse has escaped the barn? Quick! Shut the door!* While it's certainly true that the open barn door enabled the horse to escape, shutting the door now does nothing to recover the horse. In fact, given that one needs to get the horse back into the barn, shutting the door is somewhat counterproductive. Or, to stick to a medical example, imagine it's true that had a particular patient not been a smoker, she would not now have lung cancer. Although it is definitely advisable that she stop smoking now, her doing so does not *treat* her cancer. In this case, sadly, removing the cause does not address the effect.

Now consider a different case. Engaging routinely in vigorous physical exercise is a reliable way to prevent heart disease. In general, then, it's a good idea for people to exercise regularly. But once one has heart disease, vigorous physical exercise can be dangerous. In fact, if one has heart disease, engaging in the kind of physical exercise that *would have* prevented the disease is likely to cause additional damage. Here, doing what one should have been doing all along is not merely insufficient as a remedy. It actually makes things worse.

These examples raise notoriously thorny philosophical issues about causation. We needn't get entangled in those matters, as my point is simple: not all problems are of the same kind. Some can be addressed by eliminating their cause. But often there's a difference between *preventing* something from occurring and *reversing* it once it has occurred. In some cases of this latter kind, enacting measures that would have prevented the problem from arising is advisable and might even be beneficial, even though not sufficient. But in other instances, once the difficulty has arisen, introducing preventative measures is inert, or even counterproductive.

The sad fact is that when it comes to social and political dysfunctions, we often don't know what we're dealing with. The task of determining whether a given democratic failing is like iron deficiency rather than lung cancer is fraught. The matter depends on complicated empirical factors. It is safe to suppose, though, that when confronting large-scale social troubles that demand a response in the here-and-now, it's not prudent to proceed as if they're *obviously* like iron deficiency and therefore can be remediated by removing their causes. My sense is that in such cases our default assumption ought to run in the other direction. The more complex the site of the problem, the more we should expect that we are dealing with something similar to cancer rather than iron deficiency.

Thus, the *Curative Fallacy*. It is committed when one offers as the fix for a problem a course of action that would have prevented it from arising. To be more precise, the fallacy occurs when one prescribes the preventative as the curative without shouldering the empirical burden of demonstrating that the difficulty in question is of the relevant kind. It strikes me that the Curative Fallacy is especially tempting when confronting a problem where the causes are salient and independently troubling. In particularly egregious instances of the fallacy, not only is it claimed that the measures that would have prevented a defect are now the appropriate curative steps, but it is also affirmed that they are *sufficient* for remediating it. An even more extreme version holds that the preventative is *uniquely* sufficient to undo the failing.

I trust the error is straightforward enough. Here's how it is relevant for our topic. The Curative Fallacy is especially enticing when engaging in remedial democratic theory. This is because, typically, the most salient failings of democracy readily suggest clear causes. Often those causes are independently lamentable. It is hence tempting to prescribe remedial measures that eliminate those causes. My claim is that, absent further empirical details, this is an error. It's not always true that a dysfunction can be remediated by enacting the measures that would have prevented it. And sometimes enacting the preventative makes matters worse.

This remains too abstract, so consider an example. Many believe—correctly, it seems to me—that incivility poses a central problem for our democracy. For the moment, we can leave aside the question of what civility is. On any reasonable view of civility, it's plausible to think that citizens are uncivil to their partisan opponents because they have stopped listening respectfully to one another. Of course, that they have stopped listening to one another is regrettable from the democratic point of view; greater civility would definitely be an *improvement* in our democracy. But now let's grant that had citizens been engaging in practices of respectful communication all along, they would not have developed their uncivil tendencies. One might then infer that civility would be restored should citizens now adopt practices of respectful communication. Thus, an obvious prescription: in order to restore civility, citizens ought to adopt practices of respectful communication.

Despite its attraction, this line of reasoning commits the Curative Fallacy. It unwarrantedly prescribes the preventative as the curative. To be clear, just as the cancer patient ought to quit smoking, democratic citizens generally ought to adopt practices of respectful communication. That's not being denied. Yet it's not obvious that adopting those practices now will in fact counteract their current dispositions for incivility. In fact, some research suggests that under existing conditions, exposure to civil messaging from one's political opponents escalates the same negative reactions one exhibits in the presence of more overtly hostile and aggressive partisan foes.[4]

The result I just mentioned is not sufficiently robust to warrant the conclusion that adopting practices of respectful communication will *exacerbate* existing incivility. However, it does support the more modest point that, while it might be true that had we been engaging in practices of respectful communication all along we would not have to contend with elevated levels of incivility today, it does not follow that by adopting those practices now we can restore civility. To proceed otherwise is to commit the Curative Fallacy.

Once again, there are complicated issues afoot. We can leave these matters unresolved because the purpose of identifying the Curative Fallacy has not been to impeach work on democracy where it is committed. Rather, I have introduced the fallacy because it helps us to see something important about the nature of remedial democratic theory.

The Curative Fallacy indicates that our objective is not simply that of figuring out how we might have averted our current democratic dysfunctions. Although it is helpful to know the causes of polarization, the remedial task is to determine what to do next. In spelling out the Curative Fallacy, we are reminded that a description of what we should have been doing all along is not necessarily a guide to determining what we need to do now. Once we understand that the preventative is not necessarily the curative, we recognize that in order to remediate democratic failings, we might need to begin doing something other than what would have prevented them from arising. Remediating democracy might require us to do something else entirely. This book is committed to that possibility.

1.4 Democratic Theory and Democratic Politics

One final piece of scenery must be set in place before we can proceed. This book engages in democratic theory *from the inside.* Assuming that you, too, are a citizen of a democracy, we are democratic citizens engaging together in remedial theorizing about democratic citizenship. We have come to this endeavor *as citizens*, with our own political commitments and affiliations. So we enter into these reflections as advocates of particular views about what political policies are best, what the government should be doing, how the country should change, and so on. In short, you and I both are already partisans.

However, our task at present is to figure out what we, *as democratic citizens*, should do in response to the polarization dynamic. We are seeking a prescriptive account of democratic citizenship that is not itself an expression of our partisanship. The challenge, then, is to keep our partisan commitments—our *democratic politics*, if you will—distinct from our *democratic theory*. This is not easy. Some are inclined to think it's impossible. To get a sense of the difficulty, consider the following real-life vignette.

Not too long ago, I spoke to a local community organization about democracy. My presentation addressed the question of how we should conduct ourselves when disagreeing about politics. As such, it was not about any specific policy question or debate; rather, I was talking about the *ethics of citizenship*—what democratic citizens owe to one another, regardless of their partisan orientations. The talk was about democratic *theory* rather than democratic *politics*, to recall the distinction above. As far as I could tell, nothing in the presentation or the discussion with the group indicated my partisan leanings.

The conversation following the presentation went nicely, or so I thought. After the session, an audience member who had been quiet approached me with a complaint. He said, "Thanks, but I have a major problem with what you said. You see, the United

States is not a democracy. It's a republic. Everything you just said goes against the Constitution."

This was not the first time I had been presented with the claim that the United States is a republic and therefore not a democracy. My guess is that most political theorists in the United States have been reproached in this way at one time or another. As for the merits of the idea, it all depends on what one takes the terms *republic* and *democracy* to mean.

So I explained to the gentleman that the term *democracy* has shifted in meaning since the eighteenth century. At the time of the founding of the United States, those who explicitly scorned democracy took the term to denote a direct and unconstrained form of majority rule. They favored a mode government in which the majority was restricted in what it could achieve in politics. They used the term *republic* to capture the idea of constitutional government, a political order where the power of both the people and those occupying political office was limited by law. Given the ways the terms were used back then, a republic is not a democracy.

I then pointed out that hardly anyone uses these words like that today. No one who upholds democracy now embraces the idea that the majority should rule directly and without legal constraints. Rather, we today take *democracy* as the name for a representative form of constitutional government. In a democracy, the people govern themselves indirectly; they elect their fellow citizens to public office, and officials in turn are duty bound to represent the interests and priorities of their constituents in the processes of government. Importantly, all of this occurs within legal constraints set by a constitution. The United States is thus properly characterized as a *democratic republic*: constitutional self-government by the people. But, again, as hardly anyone advocates a non-republican form of democracy, it has become common to take the term *democracy* simply to mean representative and constitutional popular government.

This is a standard line among contemporary democratic theorists. But my interlocutor would have none of it. He insisted that a democracy simply is government by unconstrained mob rule, while a republic is the rule of law as set out in a constitution. He repeated that my emphasis on democracy meant that I was not committed to the US Constitution. I pointed out that the US Constitution *begins* with the claim that its validity rests with the people who "ordain and establish" it, but to no avail. He was similarly unimpressed with the point that the US Constitution opens by discussing various public offices and the rules for holding the popular elections that fill them.

In a final attempt to be conciliatory, I suggested that the dispute was simply about how to use words and not really about political theory. I added that he could work through my presentation and replace every instance of "democracy" with "republic," and I'd very likely agree with the result. But this seemed only to deepen his reservations. He responded that it is a matter of "plain English" that democracies and republics are not only distinct, but also opposed. To ensure I'd not overlook the lesson, he repeated emphatically, "and the US is a republic, not a democracy."

We parted amicably enough, but to this day I can't shake the feeling that this fellow exited the conversation thinking that I was engaging in some kind of duplicity. I got the sense that my use of the term *democracy* rather than *republic* indicated to him that I had a certain partisan bias, one that, by his lights, routinely disregards the US Constitution. Specifically, it seemed that he might have thought that my insistence that the United States is a democracy indicated an affiliation with the Democratic Party.

Thus our difficulty. A lot of our thinking about democracy focuses on what I above called democratic *politics*. When we are engaged in this kind of thinking, we seek to spell out the policy implications of our more fundamental partisan stance—what a *liberal* should think about, say, gun control, or what a properly *conservative* position on immigration would be. However, this is a book in democratic *theory*. It proposes a view about the civic responsibilities that fall to us as citizens of a democratic society, and a prescription for dealing with a specific dysfunction that we confront in that role. Accordingly, we are not here concerned with citizenship as understood from either a distinctively *liberal* or *conservative* standpoint. The aim rather is to elucidate democratic citizenship as the *framework* within which advocates of the various partisan perspectives can operate and interact. This requires that we begin our thinking from a stance above the familiar fray of our partisan divides.

I mentioned earlier, some hold that this kind of elevation is not possible. They contend that there could be no theory of democratic citizenship that is not itself the expression of some particular partisan leaning. According to this kind of view, there is no such thing as responsible democratic citizenship *per se*, but only various ideas of responsible *liberal* citizenship and responsible *conservative* citizenship. Perhaps the gentleman I encountered following my presentation to the civic group embraced this kind of position.

I think that this view is mistaken. My reasons have to do with one of its direct implications. If it is true that there is no such thing as responsible democratic citizenship as such, then it is incoherent to accuse one's political opponents of irresponsible citizenship. It strikes me that although accusations of this kind can be misplaced, it is nonetheless possible to raise a valid criticism to the effect that a partisan rival is a bad citizen or has behaved in a way that is unsuitable for a democratic citizen. The validity of such a criticism depends on there being an ideal of responsible citizenship that's not merely a restatement of our own partisan commitments. That is, if we think it's coherent to criticize others for being irresponsible citizens, we must accept that there could be a conception of good citizenship that is not itself partisan.

Still, even though I think it incorrect, the view that our conceptions of responsible citizenship are invariably partisan contains a grain of truth. Although it is possible to think about democratic citizenship from a standpoint above the partisan fray, *in fact* our thinking about citizenship tends to reflect our partisan commitments. That is, we tend to build into our idea of responsible citizenship content drawn from our own political commitments.

An intriguing experimental result suggests as much. Subjects who observe partisan opponents engaging in questionable political activity—in this case, stealing campaign signs of their favored candidate's rival off of neighbors' lawns—tend to strongly condemn the behavior as revealing a serious lapse of democratic ethics. Meanwhile, when those subjects observe that same behavior in their partisan allies, they tend to either praise it or excuse it. Apparently we think that stealing campaign signs off of neighbors' lawns is consistent with responsible citizenship, provided the signs are promoting a political rival.[5] In short, our attempts to engage in democratic theory tend to be infused with our commitments regarding democratic politics.

The lesson is that if we aim to engage here in remedial democratic theory rather than democratic politics, we need to take steps to achieve the necessary distance from our partisan perspectives. One obstacle is that democratic politics is so *familiar* to us—thinking about citizenship from the perspective of our partisan alliances and rivalries is readily at hand, and thus difficult to break away from. At the risk of trying my readers' patience, I will attempt throughout to maintain the necessary distance. At times this will require me to state what some readers might find obvious, or linger on a point that some might regard as trivial. I hope the reader can bear with me.

1.5 Sketching the Argument

With the necessary background in place, I can now sketch the path forward. In Chapter 2, I spell out the conception of democracy that underlies my claim that responsible citizenship calls for civic solitude. Picking up on some previous remarks, I will understand citizenship as a moral office characterized by two distinct civic responsibilities. On the one hand, citizens must *take responsibility for* their democracy. This requires them to engage in public collective action aimed at promoting justice as they best discern it. However, as they are political equals, citizens also have a *responsibility to* one another. This requires citizens to manifest a due regard for their fellow citizens when engaging in political advocacy. After all, democratic citizenship is not simply a matter of acting with others on behalf of one's view about what justice requires; citizenship also calls us to consider what we can rightly impose on our fellow citizens amid ongoing disagreements with them about what justice demands. As I put it earlier, democratic citizens have a responsibility to be active political participants, but their political action must also be *reflective* in ways that manifest a due consideration for their fellow citizens, including their political opponents.

Managing the dual responsibilities of democratic citizenship is tricky. Typically our political commitments reflect our considered judgments about what justice demands. We therefore are bound to regard our political opponents as advocates of injustice. Consulting with them seems not only to concede something to their viewpoint, but also to divert our energy away from the pursuit of justice. Why bother?

This question goes to the heart of democratic theory. The upshot of Chapter 2 will be that democracy's legitimacy depends not only on citizens' ability to participate as equals in political decision-making, but also on their capacity to effectively *contest* those decisions, even when they were made democratically. Once the details of this further idea are in place, we will see that we owe our fellow citizens modes of engagement that enable them to be more than *complainers* when they lose at the polls; we must uphold conditions where they can be *critics* of prevailing democratic decisions.

I will call the collection of dispositions and skills for engaging with our fellow citizens in this way *civility*. I am aware that this term is associated with the disturbing idea that citizens must always remain calm and concessive in political debate. On the account I will propose, however, civility does not require politeness or conciliation. Rather, civility involves sympathetic and imaginative reflection of a kind that enables us to regard our political opponents as critics rather than mere obstacles. That's consistent with forms of political interaction that are heated and rancorous.

Chapter 3 examines the polarization dynamic and the problem it poses for democratic citizenship. It is the most empirically dense chapter of the book. I will argue that the problem of polarization does not lie simply with escalating animosity and in-group conformity. The trouble, rather, is that when these intensifications are produced by the polarization dynamic, they tend to be based on inaccurate or false depictions of our fellow citizens and their commitments. Specifically, the polarization dynamic shrinks our conception of the range of political opinion available to responsible democratic citizens to the point where it includes only the views that we endorse. We thus come to see our political rivals as divested from democracy, ideologically beyond the pale. We adopt the stance that civility is something owed only to our allies. It goes without saying that this is a profoundly antidemocratic posture.

Counteracting these tendencies is especially difficult because the polarization dynamic functions by *centering* our partisan identities. That is, as we transform into our more extreme and conformist partisan selves, political allegiance increasingly becomes the main lens through which we situate ourselves socially. As a result, condemning our partisan rivals as unfit for democracy becomes a principal way in which we sustain social relations with our allies. Adopting a stance of civility thus often *feels like* weakness or inauthenticity. And, moreover, our allies are disposed to regard attempts to extend civility to our rivals as betrayal. That is, once the partisan self is centered, responsible democratic citizenship becomes socially risky.

More than this, the centering of the partisan self also involves what I will call the political *sorting* and *saturation* of social space. As our partisan identities are centered, more and more of what we do becomes infused with our politics. Accordingly, in the United States today, partisan affiliation is better understood as a *lifestyle* than a strictly political orientation. We will find that the cars we drive, neighborhoods we live in, television shows we watch, and clothes we wear are all heavily sorted according to partisan affiliation. It is no exaggeration to say that in the United States at least, political conservatives and liberals occupy distinct social worlds that are increasingly organized around partisan allegiance and cross-partisan hostility. Casual social interactions thus tend to occur only among those who share a partisan identity. As a consequence, our day-to-day lives reinforce the polarization dynamic.

By the end of Chapter 3, the problem to which this book is addressed will be in full view. Once again, the difficulty is that the kind of collective activity we need to engage in as democratic citizens exposes us to the polarization dynamic, which undermines our capacity for civility. The challenge is to find a way to decenter partisan identity without dissolving it, to remediate the polarization dynamic in a way that does not involve a retreat from democracy as such.

Chapter 4 presents the case for civic solitude. The details will have to wait, of course, but the driving idea is simple. Given that our social environments are already saturated with forces that center our partisan selves, counteracting the polarization dynamic requires that we occasionally exit those spaces. Should this seem an instance of the Curative Fallacy, notice that civic solitude involves more than simply removing oneself from existing social environments. In order to cultivate and restore the capacity for civility, we need to engage in a kind of *civic reflection* that is *distanced* from the partisan animus and conformity pressures produced by the polarization dynamic. The necessary reflection calls for occasions in which one can be alone, or at least momentarily secluded from the gaze of partisan allies and foes alike.

The idea of socially distanced political thinking may call to mind the image of the isolated citizen, hunched over a computer screen and doing their "own research" about matters of foreign policy, public health, climate science, and so on. Conspiracy theories and cults thrive under these conditions. One might worry, then, that civic solitude will only exacerbate existing dysfunctions.

We will return to this concern in due course. But for now, notice that the envisioned citizen doing their "own research" is not engaged in civic reflection so much as biased information mining. They are seeking out nominally reputable sources that confirm their already-held beliefs, and thus bolstering their partisan commitments in seclusion. In any case, civic solitude calls for something else. Given that its aim is to decenter the partisan self, civic solitude calls for thinking that is not only *distanced* but also *detached* from our current partisan scripts. Given how deeply ingrained these scripts tend to be, civic solitude involves the contemplation of political ideas and problems that lie beyond the terrain of our political present and that cannot be readily translated into the idiom of our partisan divides. The hope is that by extending our political vocabulary in this way we can better situate our partisan divides within an enlarged spectrum of democratic commitments.

This last point highlights another element of the case for civic solitude. Politically sorted and saturated social environments keep our attention on the immediacy of democracy—the coming election, the next policy debate, the ensuing congressional rift. The urgency of democratic politics serves to tether our thinking to the concepts that structure the politics of the moment. This inhibits the capacity to envision a democratic future that's radically different from the present, not because we've finally defeated our foes, but because the questions, problems, and division have shifted in the course of ongoing democratic politics. Civility involves maintaining the capacity to see our fellow citizens—and also ourselves—as capable of change. This requires that we take steps to decalcify the idiom and categories of our current politics, to remind ourselves that they're changeable. Reflection on political ideas and debates that not only are alien to our own circumstances, but furthermore are *not readily translatable* into our context, is crucial for cultivating the kind of political imagination that civility requires. In short, although democracy often looks like people engaging in public collective action, it *also* looks like a citizen sitting in a library or museum, confronting a style of political thought that does not apply to our contemporary political circumstances.

Chapter 4 concludes with the exploration of two important implications of the case for civic solitude. First, if a solitary mode of distanced yet civic reflection is, indeed, a component of responsible democratic citizenship, then citizens must have opportunities to engage with materials and experiences that can prompt and inform that kind of reflection. These include works of art, literature, philosophy, history, and what in educational contexts is generally understood as the Humanities. Crucially, the argument for civic solitude entails that access to material and experiences of this kind is not simply a component of a properly democratic and liberal education; it is an ongoing duty of citizenship.

Second, if occasions for civic solitude are necessary for responsible citizenship, then the sites where civic solitude could be practiced must be regarded as indispensably *democratic* spaces. This means that obvious settings for civic solitude, such as public libraries, museums, and parks, can no longer be viewed as luxuries that communities might decide to support. Rather, they are essential for democratic life, and thus citizens must have free access to them. Importantly, these are also characteristically *non-commercial* spaces. Given the ways in which partisan identity is bound up with lifestyle choices, including consumer behavior, it is essential that these spaces remain relatively free from advertisements and other commercial intrusions. In other words, these key sites for civic solitude must be publicly funded. A society's commitment to democracy requires robust investment—financial and otherwise—in public venues that are conducive to solitary civic reflection.

There's the big picture. Although the coming argument is complex, we can encapsulate it with an analogy. A popular analysis of the internet says that social media and other online phenomena threaten democracy because they allow citizens to curate their experiences. The internet enables citizens to preselect the kind of information they encounter, the voices they hear, the images they see, and ideas they come across. As a result, citizens tend to design their informational and social environments in ways that amplify their own favored perceptions. Online spaces thus function as hives in which citizens receive constant affirmation of their own perspectives. This contributes to belief polarization, which is democratically hazardous for reasons we have already identified.[6]

You're probably familiar with some version of this argument. And I'd guess that, like me, you find it generally compelling. It's true that online environments commonly function as echo chambers, where ordinary citizens are promptly angered and radicalized. Now here's the analogy: we will see that a similar assessment applies to the *offline* world. It, too, is the product of curation. Like our social media feeds, our ordinary physical environments are structured by filters that put us in touch only with people like us and perspectives that match our own. Our social world—both online and off—is an echo chamber.

One common response to the hazards posed by the internet is to urge citizens to simply log off and diversify their social and informational diet. Although the civic solitude proposal is not *identical* to this recommendation, it has a similar flavor. Our democratic pathologies are embedded in the ordinary spaces we inhabit, so in order to restore our civic capacities, we need occasionally to remove ourselves from those settings and diversify our civic intake.

1.6 Starting Small

A concluding point. Civic solitude is a mode of political engagement that we enact alone. It is a practice for citizens as *individuals*. The individualistic aspect of the proposal may provoke doubts. After all, when we think about widespread social dysfunctions, we naturally reach for large-scale mediations. We proportion our sense of the proper response to the problem's magnitude. Big problems need big solutions, we think. So when we see our democracy faltering in a big way, we reflexively look toward large-scale institutions as the source of our trouble. We explain the problem in institutional terms. We thus call for sweeping institutional change.

Civic solitude thus may seem feeble. As our account will show, polarization is pervasive. It's a large-scale democratic pathology that is arguably driven by institutions. It might seem, then, that the proper response cannot lie with individuals acting alone, but must be aimed at institutional design. That is, one might contend that civic solitude is too small to be effective against the massive problem it is supposed to address. Maybe the proposal is simply naïve.

Let's not be so hasty. Although the "big problems need big solutions" idea is intuitive, it can also mislead. When confronting large-scale social problems, it helps to keep two tasks distinct. One task is to design a comprehensive response to the problem. The other has to do with figuring out how to begin—how to *initiate* the needed changes. The "big problems need big solutions" idea can mislead because it fixes our attention on the first of these tasks, leading us to neglect the second. This in turn encourages us to think that if addressing our democratic dysfunctions calls for large-scale institutional changes, our remediation must *begin* with the institutions.

But this is an error. While it is true that a comprehensive response to polarization will likely require major institutional changes, it simply doesn't follow that our remediation efforts must begin at that scale. Sometimes the best way to initiate social reforms is to begin with modest measures. Civic solitude is a small intervention designed to *begin* to address a large-scale dysfunction. It's a way to start.

There's good reason for this "start small" approach. To put it bluntly, the project of starting with large-scale interventions is doomed. It will become clear in Chapter 3 that we cannot depend on officeholders to initiate the institutional and political changes that would help tame the polarization dynamic. This is because they benefit from the dysfunctional status quo. We will also see that, for slightly different reasons, the polarization problem cannot be taken up sufficiently by our political coalitions. We will find that polarization is a dysfunction *within* our alliances; they, too, are constructed around the very dynamics that need to be dismantled. To begin the process of restoring our civic capacities, we need to look elsewhere.

Specifically, we need to start small. A central plank of the coming argument will be that the problem of polarization is fundamentally a problem *within* each of us. We will see that, given the structure of our existing democratic ecosystem, the task of restoring our civic aptitudes falls to us as individuals. We are on our own. This is why the coming chapters do not address the large-scale and institutional interventions that might be necessary for addressing the polarization dynamic wholesale. The argument instead aims to propose something that we—*each one of us*—can try in light of where we find ourselves. Civic Solitude is a deliberately *local* prescription. But, as I emphasize in the Epilogue, this is because democracy is fundamentally a task within each of us.

So much for the stage-setting. This chapter has sketched the general contours of the view I will develop. I realize that the discussion has raised many new questions. These will be addressed along the way. For now, I hope to have at least made the idea of civic solitude more plausible than it might have seemed at the start. Of course, plausibility is a low bar. So let's begin the argument.

2
What Does Democracy Look Like?

This book proposes that there is such a thing as civic solitude, a kind of democratic activity that is necessary for good citizenship but must be practiced in isolation from others. Any view about what makes for good citizenship rests on a background idea about what democracy is all about. Accordingly, the first step in making the case for civic solitude is to clarify its underlying conception of democracy. That is the task of this chapter.

2.1 Looking for Democracy

This first step may seem easy. We all know what democracy is. We know where to find it. Thus, perhaps we can get a firm grasp on democracy by simply *looking* at it in action. Maybe we can *point* at distinctively democratic institutions and practices, say "*that's* democracy," and then discuss what makes for good citizenship. Well, things aren't that simple.

2.1.1 Democracy in the Streets

Return to the Google search for "this is what democracy looks like." The results indicate that democracy looks like masses of people gathered in a public space to voice a shared political message. As I noted earlier, this makes good sense. The images depict citizens engaging in collective political action. What's more democratic than that?

To repeat, things aren't that simple. While it is true that a thriving democracy depends on an active citizenry, the images are nonetheless politically ambiguous. To see what I mean, take a close look at your favorite photograph from the search. It's not obvious *why* individuals in the assembly are there. Perhaps we can assume that each participant is present for the sake of contributing to the collective act of political expression or engagement. But that doesn't tell us much about the democratic character of the assembly.

Here's why. Imagine discovering that the event in the photograph was staged by a powerful lobbying organization. Let's suppose the people were given cash in exchange for their participation, handed signs to carry, taught slogans to chant, and so on. Suppose further that the participants would not have shown up for the event were they not being paid. They've turned out to contribute to the collective act, but their motivation is the money, not the political expression.

Given these assumptions, what are we to make of the photograph? Surely such an assembly should be legally *permitted* in a democracy. But our question is not about the law. It is how we should assess the democratic quality of a political assembly that has been staged. We might say that such an event could make a positive contribution to democratic politics. The scripted message affirmed by the paid participants might be laudable, after all. Yet the choreographed nature of the event, along with the monetary incentive driving the citizens' involvement, diminishes the democratic character of the collective action. In short, democracy *doesn't* look like amateur actors paid to perform the role of engaged citizens.

We could press this evaluation further. It is plausible to think that when collective political action is monetized and scripted by powerful political agents working behind the scenes, the result is *counterfeit* democracy. Such imitations are pernicious. They're typically designed to manipulate the larger citizenry into thinking that a particular political sentiment is more widespread than it in fact is. In certain contexts, staged mass public political action is a characteristic form of populist propaganda, which is typically antidemocratic.[1] Hence we might see fit to *blame* the participants for contributing to a forgery of democracy. In any case, under the assumptions we have introduced, the image depicts people *playing* at citizenship, not exercising it.[2]

It seems, then, that images of citizens engaging together in public collective political expression depict *democracy* only when it is supposed that the participants (or enough of them, at any rate) have certain motivations and not others. To put things roughly, we could say that episodes of collective political action manifest democracy insofar as the participants are motivated by the political sentiments that their public activity aims to express. Their contributions to the collective action must be *authentic* or *sincere*, so to speak. When we look at the returns of the Google search and think that they, indeed, are depictions of democracy, we are implicitly projecting onto the participants certain civic motivations.

Now consider a different scenario. Take another look at your favorite photograph from the image search. Assume that the participants weren't paid, and indeed are motivated by the political sentiments that their collective action expresses. Still, this is not enough to render their collective action exemplary of democracy. Imagine that most of them hold wildly false—even irrational—views regarding the issue on whose behalf they are acting. Just to fix ideas, suppose that the photograph shows a large number of citizens protesting a specific immigration policy that their government has recently enacted. But also assume that most of the protesters can't accurately describe the policy they're demonstrating against. Or, to make the problem more salient, stipulate that the majority of the protesters believe that the policy in question imposes stricter immigration restrictions, while it in fact loosens them. The protesters are demonstrating in opposition to a policy that they would favor but for their ignorance.

As with our previous example, we can say that such an assembly should be legally permitted and might even be in some sense democratically beneficial (again, the protesters might be unwittingly opposing a bad policy). Nevertheless, it involves a democratic shortcoming on the part of the citizens. Although they have the right motivation for their participation in collective democratic action, they're so radically ignorant of certain relevant facts that their joint activity seems irredeemably *irrational*. We might be tempted to say that the group doesn't really *act* at all—it is too haphazard to count as doing anything in particular. But we can set that idea aside. Our question is what we should make of the photograph under the assumption that the participants are drastically misinformed. Is *that* what democracy looks like?

According to democracy skeptics, that *is* what democracy looks like! These critics hold that when it comes to politics, citizens are irredeemably foolish and irrational. They contend that democracy therefore should be opposed, or at least supplemented with new institutions and practices designed to empower experts and disarm the ignorance of the people.

While widespread political ignorance is indeed a problem in modern democracies, we need not examine the democracy skeptics' arguments here. We are not asking whether one should endorse democracy instead of some alternative. Nor are we raising the question of whether such radical political ignorance could disqualify persons from being citizens. And, again, we are not concerned with the *legality* of the citizens' behavior. Rather, our concern has to do with the democratic credentials of various instances of collective political action. We are considering a public demonstration conducted by citizens who are profoundly mistaken about the target of their protest.

Such thoroughgoing misunderstanding on the part of the citizens diminishes the democratic character of their collective activity. Though I believe this assessment to be correct, it raises a difficulty. On the one hand, our example suggests that there is a point at which citizens' ignorance undercuts their capacity to act together democratically. On the other hand, we cannot expect democratic citizens to be experts on all matters of public policy. Responsible citizenship calls for a certain degree of political *competence*; but the requirements for responsible citizenship must be within reach for ordinary people. Accordingly, some degree of political ignorance must be consistent with the kind of competence citizens need if they are to be responsible democratic participants.

The difficulty lies in identifying the level of competence that citizens need to attain. Democracy skeptics hold that ordinary citizens fall short of any reasonable standard of political competence, while democracy's defenders hold that citizens can be competent to the required degree.[3] The issue is vexed. However, we can sidestep debates over the details of political competence. The point at present is one that nearly everyone accepts: when political *incompetence* is especially pronounced, citizens' collective activities seem no longer democratic in a laudable sense of the term. If the current case doesn't strike you as involving a sufficiently severe degree of ignorance, imagine a different scenario that does.

Let's get back to the example at hand. Given details about the ease with which the relevant political information could have been accessed, we might *fault* the participants for their incompetence; we might hold that they should have known better. Or, in light of additional assumptions, we might chalk their ignorance up to some other failure such as bigotry or intolerance. There might even be circumstances under which we would regard the participants as *victims* of the misinformation they have embraced.

In any case, democracy *doesn't* look like severely ignorant people assembled in public space to communicate a political message that they profoundly misunderstand. Thus, in addition to having appropriate motivations, citizens must also achieve a certain level of competence if their political activity is to exemplify democracy.

I leave it to the reader to devise additional scenarios along the lines of the two we have discussed. Indeed, we could continue in this way for a rather long time, introducing various assumptions about the participants in the photographs that undercut the democratic character of their collective activity. The fact that we could go on like this is noteworthy, as it reveals something significant about our ordinary understandings of democracy and citizenship. The foregoing discussion has suggested that absent certain motives and competencies among the citizens, collective political action loses its democratic luster. Accordingly, when we imagine that the citizens are profoundly ignorant or motivated strictly by money, it's difficult to see their collective public action as manifesting democracy in the laudatory sense that would warrant the reaction "*that* is what democracy looks like." Absent the relevant motives and competence, a crowd of people acting together on behalf of a political message looks like a mob.

This indicates that whether citizens' collective political action counts as exemplifying democracy depends largely on certain facts about *them*: what prompted them to participate, what information they have, how they arrived at their stance on the issues, and so on. Democracy happens in public spaces, but so does a lot else, including many modes of politics that involve episodes of mass public action but nonetheless are not democratic. The difference between a collective act of democracy and some other kind of public political performance can depend on what the citizens bring to the enterprise. In this sense, democracy depends on what goes on inside of us.

That strikes me as an instructive result. Yet we must take care not to overstate it. I am not suggesting that under the proposed assumptions, the Google images depict *antidemocratic* activity. Rather, I have been pressing the more modest claim that when we stipulate that the citizens are grossly incompetent or not properly motivated, it's not clear what to say about their collective action. It's not *obvious* that their joint activity is democratic in an exemplary sense. This shows that democracy is not strictly a matter of collective political participation. It has also to do with what's behind our actions, with our *dispositions*.

Democratic citizenship thus involves a *civic ethos*—a distinctive collection of attitudes, skills, habits, and practices that responsible citizens routinely bring to bear on their political advocacy. An ethos can't be captured in a photograph. It can't really be *seen*. Thus, the images returned in the Google search are politically ambiguous. Taken at face value, they don't depict democracy after all. To see "what democracy looks like," we need to look beneath the surface.

2.1.2 Democracy in the Voting Booth

Consider another popular place that we might look to when thinking about democracy. Conduct a Google Images search for the term *democracy*. This will return thousands of pictures of people engaging various activities—raising a hand, standing in line at a polling station, pulling a lever, checking a box, casting a ballot, and so on. The depicted activities are all associated with *voting*.

This makes good sense. When thinking about democracy, we intuitively fix on its characteristic institutions. Elections, voting, campaigns, and public offices naturally come to mind. We tend to define democracy *institutionally*. We say it is a form of government where the people rule by voting in elections that select their political representatives.[4]

This is a fine way to proceed in many contexts. Elections indeed are central to modern democracies. In fact, they are often regarded as *necessary* for democracy.[5] When one is trying to determine whether an unfamiliar country is democratic, it hence makes good sense to look to see whether it conducts routine popular elections. However, we are not deciding whether some particular country is a democracy. We are rather trying to figure out what democracy is all about, so that we may discern the responsibilities of democratic citizenship. And it turns out that the institutional definition doesn't get us very far. This is because institutions are manifestations of the values and purposes they are designed to realize.

To see this, consider a definition of a bicycle that attends strictly to its definitive components. For example, one might say that a bicycle is an object with two wheels, two pedals, a handlebar with two grips, one frame, one chain, one seat. Such an account would leave one wondering why some components come in twos, while others are singular. In order to explain the structure of the bicycle, one needs to mention the fact that a bicycle is a mode of human transport. In the absence of a description of the bicycle's *purpose*, even an exhaustive explanation of the bicycle's parts is inadequate.

The same goes for democracy. If we seek to understand it, we can't look only at the machinery that makes it run. We need also to identify what those institutions are *for*, what they are meant to achieve. If we say that electoral institutions are designed to achieve *democracy*, we thereby affirm that democracy is something distinct from the institutions that realize it. Accordingly, to understand what democracy is, we need to look to the purposes that underwrite its institutions. We need to look beneath the surface.

Although this result may seem intuitive, the institutional approach to understanding democracy remains entrenched in our thinking. So it is worth taking a moment to elaborate.

There's a clear sense in which democracy is a form of government where the people rule by voting in elections. Yet that analysis is incomplete until we explain how elections are structured in a democratic society. Specifically, we would need to say why properly democratic elections are fair and open. We would need to clarify why an election where it is illegal to vote against the sitting officeholder is not democratic. Likewise, we would need to account for the fact that elections fail to be democratic when only the members of the ruling party are permitted to run for office, or when only the votes supporting a particular candidate count. There are many ways in which an election can fail to be democratic, after all. So, when we point to elections as definitive of democracy, we are always referencing elections that have features that *make* them democratic. This provokes the question of why those features are necessary for an election to be democratic.

We cannot address this new question by pointing to some other core democratic fixture—the constitution, the legal system, legislative procedures, or what have you. That would only prompt one to ask why *those* institutions function as they do, thus merely relocating the initial question. Nor can we identify democracy with the *collection* of its characteristic institutions—the *system* of open and fair elections, constitutionally constrained representative legislatures, an independent judiciary, and so on. That only raises the question of what makes that system democratic. Instead, one needs to identify the purposes that those institutions are supposed to serve, the goods they are meant to realize. Hence our conclusion: democracy isn't simply a form of government composed of characteristic institutions; rather, it is more fundamentally the values that underlie those institutions.

To repeat, there's more to democracy than meets the eye. The foregoing considerations show that democracy is neither its characteristic modes of collective action, nor its distinctive institutions. If we want to explain the centrality of those forms of participation and institutions, we can't take democracy at face value. We can't find democracy by simply *looking*. Instead, we must get beneath democracy's familiar practices and institutions. We must identify its underlying values.

2.2 Democracy as a Social Ideal

To understand democracy, we need to treat it as a *social ideal*. Specifically, we need to regard democracy as the ideal of a *self-governing society of equals*. In this sense, democracy is an *aspiration*. It does not describe some specific society. It rather advances a vision of a properly arranged political order. The significance of democracy being an aspiration will be discussed at the end of this chapter. Our task at present is to spell out the content of the democratic ideal.

The first thing to note is that democracy makes the claim that it is *possible* for us to live together as equals. It is the thesis that ordinary people are able to sustain a decent political order in the absence of royals, overlords, nobles, and masters. Democracy is the dignifying proposal that it is possible for us to live together without anyone calling the shots for everyone else. It contends that we can govern ourselves together on equal terms.

Because democracy is so familiar to us, we tend to overlook the fact that it is a radical proposal. We regard it as commonplace, humdrum. But there's nothing ordinary about the democratic ideal. For one thing, it stands in defiance of the most common political forms that have prevailed in human history, all of which are rooted in the claim that ordinary people must be ruled by their betters. Democracy hence is a *historically* notable idea. But that's not all. Democracy is also *conceptually* distinctive. To repeat, it affirms that it is *possible* for us to live together as equals. This core claim is not as obviously true as one might suppose. If we want a clear sense of the democratic ideal, then, we need to get a feel for its conceptual novelty.

2.2.1 *Can We Live Together as Equals?*

Is a decent political order possible among equals? There is good reason to think it might not be. To see this, begin with the observation that politics is a matter of establishing the conditions under which we live together. When it comes to our interactions with most other people, the things that we must do, are prohibited from doing, and are permitted to do are largely matters of politics. This much is obvious. But once we adopt the additional premise that we are equals, a problem arises. Part of what it means to be equals is that we are not required to surrender our judgment to anyone else.

We each get to make up our own minds. To be sure, there are limits on what we are permitted to *do*. But, within those constraints, we each get to live on our own terms. And in any case no one gets to dictate what we must *believe*. As a result, we are likely to disagree about the specific shape our life together should take.

Given this upshot of our equality, it follows that politics necessarily involves the exercise of power by some over others. And that is exactly what governments do. They enforce rules that compel people to do what they otherwise would not do, do not want to do, would prefer not to do, do not think they should be forced to do, and so on. They *impose* order. We can say that a government is a system of social control amid ongoing disagreement. Any such system appears to violate equality, as it forces some to comply with rules that they do not endorse, to live on terms that are not their own. Thus, it seems that we cannot live together as equals.

Some readers will have noticed that a variety of anarchism is lurking.[6] This view holds that politics in any form is a matter of forcing people to get in line. Hence, the anarchist claims, politics as such *subordinates* some while enabling others to dominate. As relations of subordination and domination are paradigmatically *unequal* relations, the anarchist concludes that no political order is possible among equals. As the anarchist also affirms that persons are indeed equals, the conclusion is that no form of politics can be justified. Thus, the core anarchist contention: no matter how they may be structured, governments are fundamentally illegitimate.

Regardless of what one thinks of anarchism as a philosophical stance, the argument sketched above serves as a compelling foil. It brings into relief an easily overlooked tension between equality and the project of maintaining a political order. What's key for our purposes is that this tension is *conceptual*. In other words, the difficulty is not that people are too corrupt or selfish to live together as equals; the concern isn't that we're not able to *live up to* the task. The anarchist's point rather is that politics *necessarily* imposes inequality. If this is correct, we cannot live together as equals, because living together in a political order—even a perfectly democratic one—is inherently hierarchical.

Now, one might respond to the anarchist by denying that people are equals. This is how traditional arguments for aristocracy proceed.[7] They begin from the premise that certain people are entitled to lord over others in virtue of being *better* in some specified sense. Another kind of response holds that when politics is conducted properly, no exercises of coercive power are necessary. This view—call it *social holism* (admittedly the term is not ideal)—maintains that people are indeed equals, but then contends that when society is justly arranged, everyone lives together in harmonious unanimity.[8] As such, social holists regard conflict and disagreement as a *failure* of politics.

There's a lot more to say about both positions. But notice that neither really responds to the anarchist's concerns; rather, they *dodge* them. Aristocracy and social holism seek to render the anarchist argument moot. Both views assert that in a properly structured political order, there is no such tension as the one that anarchism identifies, either because people aren't equals, or because politics doesn't require coercion.

The conceptual innovation of democracy now comes into focus. The democrat meets the anarchist head-on. With the anarchist, the democrat asserts both that persons are equals *and* that politics always involves the exercise of coercive power. Yet the democrat rejects the anarchist conclusion. Against the anarchist, the democrat contends that one can be *subjected* to coercive power without thereby being *subordinated* by it. In other words, the democrat holds that one can be coerced and yet retain one's equality. Specifically, the democrat asserts that when political power is exercised democratically, coercion is *non-subordinating*. If this is correct, anarchism is false. We can live together as equals after all.

I said earlier that democracy is a dignifying proposal. Yet it must be admitted that the very idea of non-subordinating coercion is peculiar. Moreover, the corresponding claim that one can be subjected to coercive power without being subordinated by it is not immediately plausible. To make sense of the idea that coercive power can be exercised among equals, we need to examine the conception of equality that lies at the core of the democratic ideal.

2.2.2 Equal Standing

We have identified democracy with the ideal of a self-governing society of equals. What does this equality come to? We should note straightaway that claiming that people are equals does not mean that they are all the same, always deserving of equivalent treatment, or identically meritorious. Rather, democracy proposes that people have *equal standing*. This idea has both moral and political aspects.

On the moral side, equal standing means that we each embody our own distinctive perspective and have our own life to live. It is the idea we each occupy a unique standpoint within the world and, for better or worse, bring our own judgment to bear on where we find ourselves. This uniqueness means that we are each *responsible* for our conduct, and no one's life is simply disposable or of utterly no regard. This in turn means that no one is merely an instrument for another's purposes or an object for another's use. In short, the moral dimension of our equal standing entails that, from the moral point of view, *everyone matters*. It follows that insofar as there are differences in the moral significance we assign to people, those differences call for justification. No one can be simply discounted.

When it comes to politics, equal standing is the affirmation of *antihierarchy*.[9] The democrat denies that people inherently stand toward one another in relations of inferiority and superiority. Equality means that no one is by nature another's overlord, pawn, master, or lackey. This means, again, that insofar as individuals *do* stand in such relations to one another, those arrangements must be justified. Thus, no citizen is *politically* another's lesser, and everyone has a presumptive entitlement to live on their own terms within the constraint of respecting others' entitlement to live on *their* own terms.[10]

I trust that this much is commonplace. Things get more interesting with the observation that there is no way to be an equal all by oneself. This is because equal standing is fundamentally a *relation* among people. In asserting our equality, then, we thereby also affirm the equality of others—we recognize them as *our* equals. Although the grammar may be strained, to assert one's equal standing is at the same time to assert one's *equality with* others, or at least *some* of them. But notice how this point expands. A moment's reflection shows that the bases upon which we affirm our equal standing with specific others are not, after all, unique to us. The same considerations we appeal to in asserting our equality are available to everyone else as grounds for *their* equal standing. Thus we arrive at a core commitment of democracy: we all matter, and no one is another's political subordinate. We can encapsulate this idea by saying that democratic citizens stand as *one another's equals*.[11]

Consider a further consequence. Our equal standing means that no one gets to call the shots for everyone else. Therefore, insofar as we seek to live together as equals at all, each of us must acknowledge that we can't always get our way. The very prospect of living in a political order with our equals *requires* that we will sometimes have to comply with rules that we do not endorse and perhaps even oppose. Our fellow citizens will exercise their own judgment and come to their own ideas about the particular shape our common life should take. Recognizing their equal standing involves reconciling ourselves to the fact that we cannot simply boss everyone else around. Democracy is the thesis that reconciling ourselves to this fact need not involve relinquishing our equality. Indeed, democracy invokes the further claim that we *recognize* the equality of others by trying to live with them in a democratic order.

2.2.3 Coercion without Subordination

We can now make sense of the idea of non-subordinating coercion. What matters for equality is not whether we are subjected to coercive power, but rather the character of the processes by which that power is constrained and directed. Specifically, democracy claims that citizens retain their equality despite being subject to coercive power when they have an equal say in deciding how power will be deployed *and* needn't simply resign in the wake of its exercise.

Notice that this contention has two parts. The first invokes the familiar idea of democracy that prevails in the schoolyard. It says that that in order for coercion to be non-subordinating, each person subject to it must be able to participate as an equal in deciding how it will be exercised. This idea is undeniably plausible. When we each get an equal say in directing power, no one gets to call the shots for everyone else. However, the schoolyard view is not complete until we specify an additional characteristic. Not only must we each have an equal voice in the decision-making process, but the collective outcome must reflect a *fair* accounting of what each of us says. Majority rule is in most contexts a *fair* way to transfer the multiple equal inputs into a single output. For that reason, it serves as the democratic default, deviation from which stands in need of justification.

It is common to treat the schoolyard view as an adequate conception of democracy. Yet it's easy to see why ultimately it is not enough. After all, one can have equal input into the decision to permanently disenfranchise or otherwise oppress a small minority of which one is a member. Equal input into fair decision-making processes thus is not sufficient to secure equal standing. To understand how one can be coerced without being subordinated, then, we must introduce the idea that in a democracy, there are *constraints* on what political majorities can achieve, even by means of democratic processes. These are often articulated as civil rights—entitlements that individuals have *regardless* of the majority will (and sometimes *against* it). In the context of the United States, we think of the Bill of Rights as establishing such constraints.

Political philosophers tend to treat these limits as defining the scope of individual liberty, the areas of life where one is not accountable to anyone else and thus shielded from intrusion. The idea is that our liberty begins where politics ends. However, our purposes draw attention to the fact that these entitlements also serve a political—and decidedly *democratic*—function. They establish conditions under which citizens can *preserve* their equal standing even when they find themselves on the losing end of a political decision. Our civil rights, then, are tools by which we *retain* our equality throughout the course of democratic politics. They serve not simply as protections from political interference, but also as means by which we can stand up for ourselves in the political arena. Because of these entitlements, you may lose at the polls without losing your voice.

Thus the second part of the democrat's thesis: coercive power is non-subordinating provided that one needn't *resign* in the wake of its exercise. The idea is that in a democracy, even when one gets outvoted, one need not simply *acquiesce* in the result. Citizens can critique democratic outcomes—they can object to them, challenge them, and in some ways even *resist* them—without thereby abandoning democracy. Furthermore, in the wake of a democratic defeat, likeminded citizens can band together, form coalitions, raise money, and *demonstrate* in opposition to the prevailing outcome. To be sure, when a collective decision is reached by democratic processes, citizens generally must comply; however, they are never required to do so *quietly*. No democratic outcome is *final*; self-government among equals is an ongoing project. Thus, even when a decision has resulted from an impeccably democratic process, citizens always have *recourse*. Democracy means never having to shut up.

Political contestation thus is built into the office of democratic citizenship. And this is vital to our equality. In a democracy, we do not only get an equal say; we also get to exercise our voice after a decision has been reached. We are entitled to persist in our dissent. We are empowered to address our fellow citizens as well as our elected officials and call for a change to existing policies, even when they enjoy widespread support. Crucially, these contestatory activities *assert* our equality. Even when we find ourselves on the losing side of a democratic decision, we nonetheless have access to channels by which we affirm our standing as equal partners in self-government.

The democrat's view can be encapsulated in the following way. Coercive power is non-subordinating when it is directed, constrained, and contestable by the people who are subjected to it. Note how this analysis of how coercive power can be non-subordinating makes sense of the two Google searches discussed earlier. Elections are central means by which citizens express their equal say in political decision-making, while collective public action is paradigmatic of political contestation. When we think of a political order in which citizens have equal input in deciding the terms under which they live together, but also have access to channels by which they can contest those terms after the votes are counted, we instinctively think *that's* democracy. We now see that this reaction is based on the idea that practices associated with voting and public contestation are manifestations of the underlying value of creating a political order that is fit for equals. This is an order in which every citizen counts, even after every vote is counted.

2.3 What Citizens Owe to One Another

We are now able to get beneath democracy's surface. The discussion has shown that a democracy is a society in which citizens not only *direct* power as equals, but also are able to *contest* the exercise of power even when it has been directed by democratic processes.

In both ways, democratic citizenship has to do with exercises of power among equals. As the anarchist is keen to remind us, this is a morally weighty enterprise. Thus, unless the task of directing power is taken up with the proper moral sensibility, politics turns out to be exactly what the anarchist alleges, namely the brute subordination of our equals. Although the institutional channels by which power is directed and contested are complex and often indirect, it nonetheless falls to us as citizens to ensure the democratic character of our politics. In a democracy, the buck stops with us.

That suggests that democracy has to do with what goes on inside of us. It is a matter of what we bring to the enterprise of directing and evaluating exercises of political power in light of the fact that our fellow citizens are our equals. In other words, democratic citizenship is a *moral office*. It invokes a civic ethos—a collection of dispositions, competencies, and practices that citizens must bring to the project of collective self-government among equals. We thus can identify the *responsibilities* of citizenship, requirements for enacting our civic role in ways that duly respect the equal standing of our fellow citizens. In falling short of these responsibilities, we contribute to a political order that subordinates our equals.

It is important to emphasize that these responsibilities reflect what we owe to our fellow citizens. Of course, some of our fellow citizens are also our friends, siblings, neighbors, co-workers, and so on. Those relations give rise to their own distinctive duties. But our present concern is with what we owe to others in our civic roles, strictly as democratic citizens.

It should be added that democratic citizenship might also give rise to responsibilities of other kinds. One might argue, for instance, that democratic citizens owe distinctive duties specifically to their country; these are typically called *patriotic* duties. There may also be *intergenerational* duties that democratic citizens owe to long-deceased political forebears, or to distant future generations—roughly, persons who are either no longer or not yet citizens. But our focus is more limited. We are interested in the responsibilities we bear toward our fellow citizens in the here-and-now, given our shared status as equal partners in democratic self-government.

It is important to note that the responsibilities we are concerned with are moral rather than legal. In identifying them, we are not establishing conditions for *unlawful* behavior. We rather are devising a conception of proper civic conduct, a view of *good* citizenship. These responsibilities help us to identify ways that we can treat our fellow citizens well or badly in a distinctively political sense. And it is by reference to them that we can be admirable or deficient in our civic behavior.[12] These responsibilities thus capture what citizens owe *to one another*. To keep things tidy, we can call them *civic* responsibilities of democratic citizenship.

We can now cut to the heart of the matter. We have seen that democratic citizenship invokes two related civic tasks. Citizens must govern together as equals, while also recognizing one another's equality. These two tasks supply the basis for our civic responsibilities. Specifically, they underwrite three interrelated components of responsible citizenship. In governing together as equals, citizens must be *public-minded*; and in order to recognize one another's equality, citizens must engage together in ways that are both *responsive* and *transparent*. Taken as a package, these requirements form an overall conception of responsible democratic citizenship, what I will call the democratic ethos of *civility*.

2.3.1 Public-Mindedness

Let's start with the task of governing together as equals. This means that we must *take responsibility for* our democracy. We have a duty to uphold democratic institutions and norms that enable us to govern together as equals. Upholding these institutions involves participating in the processes of self-government, and not free-riding on others' democratic labor. In short, one way in which we help to secure political conditions under which citizens can govern together as equals is to contribute our own voice to the processes of democratic self-government. As the saying goes, democracy depends on a vigilant citizenry. And vigilance calls for political participation.

But that's not all there is to governing together as equals. When we are deciding *how* to exercise our voice—whether by voting, protesting, campaigning, or advocating in some other way—our objective cannot be simply to get our own way, serve our own advantage, or overcome our foes. Instead, our advocacy must reflect a sincere attempt to discern what *justice* calls for rather than what serves our particular interests. Otherwise we are attempting to game the democratic process in order to force others to live on our terms.

To put this point positively, governing together as equals invokes the responsibility to promote justice as we best can discern it, *given that we are members of a society of equals*. To do this, not only must we acquire political information and process it in a competent way. Promoting justice requires also that we adopt a *public* perspective. When it comes to deciding how coercive power will be exercised among our equals, justice is not simply a matter of what we, from our own point of view, think is best. The task of promoting justice within a society of equals requires us to take a broader stance. We must try to discern what is best given that our fellow citizens embrace values and priorities that might not align with our own. So in order to promote justice within a democracy, the question we must ask is not what justice requires simply from our own evaluative perspective, but rather what we can justly impose on our equals in light of the fact that they have their own ideas about what justice requires. To put it somewhat dramatically, governing together as equals involves the attempt to pursue justice amid ongoing disagreements with one's equals over what justice requires.

Thus, democratic citizens have the responsibility to promote justice by seeking a *common* good, what's best for *us* as a community of self-governing equals. Part of taking responsibility for our democracy consists in advocating for policies and decisions that can plausibly be regarded as *acceptable* (even if not *optimal*) to our fellow citizens because they are rooted in a due consideration of their own values and priorities. To govern together as equals, then, democratic citizens must be *public-minded*. In their pursuit of justice, they not only must be politically active; they must also be both competent and motivated to pursue a common good.

2.3.2 Responsiveness and Transparency

This brings us to the second civic task. Democratic citizens must recognize one another as their equals. This means that citizens must act in ways that are *responsible to* their fellow citizens. They must regard their fellow citizens not merely as people who *get* equal input into decision-making processes, but rather as democratic partners who are *entitled* to an equal political voice. This mode of civic responsibility has two intertwined aspects; call them *responsiveness* and *transparency*.

Begin with responsiveness. When we are deciding how to exercise our political voice, we must do more than acquire *data* about our fellow citizens' perspectives. Regarding them as our equals requires that we treat them as something more than obstacles around which we must strategize. We recognize the equality of our fellow citizens by giving their perspectives *due consideration*. Our political views must take account of our fellow citizens' values and priorities, including their criticisms of our ideas. We must try to understand their views and what drives them; our own views must be *informed* by theirs. We must formulate our own political views in ways that reflect a sincere encounter with the views of our fellow citizens. Indeed, this kind of engagement is necessary for *public-mindedness*; in order to discern the common good, we need to grasp what our fellow citizens value and how they think. In any case, acknowledging our fellow citizens' equality requires that we be *responsive* to their points of view.

To be clear, responsiveness does not mean that each citizen must consult with every other. That would be absurd, even were it possible. Although some degree of face-to-face engagement among citizens is necessary for democracy, responsiveness is more typically achieved by means of highly mediated democratic channels, including the Press, political commentators, political parties, and public-interest associations. The key to being responsive is to form one's political judgments in light of an assessment of the variety of ideas and perspectives that prevail among our fellow citizens.

Yet responsiveness is not all there is to acknowledging our fellow citizens' equality. Recall that in order for coercion to be nonsubordinating, citizens must be able to *contest* political decisions, even when they have been made democratically. Recognizing our fellow citizens as our equals hence has to do with *remaining open* to their disputation even after a democratic decision has been reached. Citizens must acknowledge that although elections and other democratic processes result in decisions with which everyone must comply, they don't exactly *settle* anything. Not once and for all, at any rate. So it's not enough to consult fellow citizens when deciding how to vote or advocate, we must also be prepared to *revisit* political questions in light of the objections of our fellow citizens.

Think of it this way. Familiar democratic entitlements *enable* citizens to speak out against standing policies. But in order for that kind of political activity to count as *contestation*, it must be able to reach an audience that is socially positioned to make a difference. Otherwise, acts of critique and protest are cases of mere *complaining*. Citizens of a self-governing society of equals thus owe it to one another to sustain conditions under which those who find themselves on the losing side of a decision can do more than merely *complain* about it. Aggrieved citizens must be able to address their objections to the democratic public; their contestation must potentially have *uptake*. And we, as their equal partners in democracy, must be prepared to give their criticisms a hearing.

Consider a further implication. When understood as a means for recognizing one another's equality, contestation is a *reason-governed* activity; it advances a *critique* rather than a brute demand or threat. I realize that this may sound strange. When we think of political contestation, we intuitively envision mass public action involving various forms of resistance and overt noncompliance. Our minds do not turn to settings in which people reason together. However, barring certain dire political contexts, noncompliance with a democratically decided policy is not itself an act of contestation. Unless noncompliance is accompanied by a message or claim that serves as a *criticism* of standing conditions, it is at best an exercise of oppositional force. To be clear, there are conditions under which that kind of noncompliance is justified within a democracy; and in extreme cases it might even be obligatory. However, the modes of contestatory action that embody citizens' equal standing must involve a *critique* of existing policies, not simply their *rejection*. Thus, contestation trades in *reasons*. It must address one's fellow citizens in ways that they can *evaluate* and respond to, perhaps with defenses of the status quo.

This latter point is crucial. In order for contestation to function as critique rather than as a raw demand, it must trade in reasons of a particular kind. Specifically, contestation must express reasons that are accessible to our fellow citizens; they must be in this sense *public*. These are reasons of a kind that we can expect our fellow citizens to recognize as addressed to the public good, again in light of the fact that we each are equals with our own overall perspectives.

That is, our contestation must advance concerns and objections that are formulated in terms of core democratic ideals, such as equality, autonomy, freedom, and dignity. Meanwhile, characteristically *non-accessible* reasons draw strictly from one's own specific evaluative perspective—the values, priorities, and objectives that one embraces, but which other citizens need not share. Political critique that is formulated in terms that belong only to our own perspective gives our fellow citizen no basis for evaluation and response. For that reason, although critique of that kind may be permissible in a democratic society, it does not qualify as the kind of contestation that is essential for maintaining equal standing and that commands an audience of one's fellow citizens. In short, the reasons driving democratic contestation must be *transparent* to our fellow citizens.

Transparency is a two-way street. Contestation must proceed by way of reasons that are accessible to the general democratic public. But that means that the underlying rationale for standing democratic policies must also be publicly accessible. Citizens must be able to critically engage with and respond to the reasons that are alleged to support the policies they seek to contest. In this way, transparency involves the requirement to conduct one's political thinking in a democratic idiom, not only to participate in a *public-minded* way, but also to think in terms of considerations that are accessible to one's fellow citizens.

Notice that neither responsiveness nor transparency calls for citizens to be concessive in the face of disagreement. Recognizing the equal standing of our fellow citizens does not require us to adopt the view that our political opponents might be correct. Nor does it require us to always seek the middle ground in political debate. It might be good to take that kind of open-minded stance, of course. But it is not a requirement of good citizenship. Responsiveness and transparency are satisfied in virtue of our being able to engage in ongoing democratic disputation on questions of the common good in ways that are informed by what our fellow citizens actually believe. The responsibilities of responsiveness and transparency reflect the idea that we recognize our fellow citizens' equal standing when we *go to the source* in trying to understand them. That does not require us to modulate our conflicts or cede political ground. Rather, responsiveness and transparency render our political rifts democratically authentic.

Finally, it must also be emphasized that responsiveness and transparency do not jointly entail the implausible view that citizens are required to give a hearing to fellow citizens' perspectives *no matter what*. In any free society, there will be some citizens who embrace political viewpoints that are at odds with the democratic ideal. Affirming such views typically calls into question one's fitness for citizenship. In extreme cases, holding certain political beliefs is even *disqualifying* for good-standing membership in a democratic society. Proponents of some such perspectives are undeserving of any engagement whatsoever. To be sure, the question of what—if anything—we owe to citizens whose views are beyond the pale is important. But that question can be answered only once we have a clear sense of what we owe to our fellow citizens whose views are *not* beyond the pale, but merely wrong. After all, not all political ideas that conflict with our own are beyond the pale; moreover, having correct political beliefs is not a requirement for being a democratic citizen in good standing. In a self-governing society of equals, we each have to recognize that there is a large class of political opinions that are false, but nonetheless within bounds.

In any case, the account on offer concerns the responsibilities we have toward our fellow citizens in good standing. Affirming that we owe them advocacy and engagement that is public-minded, responsive, and transparent is consistent with the standard range of views concerning what—again, if anything—responsible citizens owe to those whose commitment to democracy is seriously in doubt. Surely ideas and commitments that contradict the democratic ideal must be opposed, and there will be cases where that opposition must involve measures other than responsiveness and transparency. Still, the matter of how responsible democratic citizens should treat those among their fellows who hold political views that are beyond the pale is simply a different question from the one we are addressing here.

2.3.3 Civility

Before fitting these pieces together, let's take a moment to review. If we are to be good citizens, we must *take responsibility for* our democracy while also acknowledging our *responsibility to* our fellow citizens. We must be active participants in democracy while also duly recognizing the equality of our civic partners. I have suggested that our political advocacy thus must be public-minded, responsive, and transparent. That is, we must seek justice as a *common* good, while also taking account of our fellow citizens' perspectives and standing ready to revisit democratic decisions in light of their contestation.

Observe that, in the abstract at least, these three components of responsible citizenship are mutually supporting. In order to advocate in ways that are public-minded, we need to access our fellow citizens' concerns and priorities; this means we must engage together in ways that are responsive and transparent. And in advocating for public-minded policies, we enrich the social channels through which citizens can govern together responsively and transparently. To reflect the interlocking structure of these responsibilities, we can refer to them collectively as the democratic ethos of *civility*. Hence, as a shorthand we can say that what democratic citizens owe to one another is civility.

2.3.3.1 Civility as a Norm of Recognition

The term "civility" is fraught.[13] It is encumbered with connotations of reconciliation and compromise. On common understandings, civility requires that we make peace with our political opposition, or always deescalate our conflicts with them. As many have argued, civility in this sense is objectionable. Specifically, understood as a norm of reconciliation, civility is a recipe for *appeasement*. It thus cedes a strategic advantage to those who are most ruthless and powerful by enabling them to determine the middle ground and thus set the terms of compromise. So understood, civility favors the existing balance of political power, and thus the status quo.

This critique is well placed. When understood as a norm of reconciliation, civility is not required for responsible citizenship. However, according to the view that we have been developing, civility is not a stance of concession and accord. To repeat, it is a set of dispositions, competencies, and habits that serve to acknowledge the equality of our fellow citizens amid political difference. In general, then, civility as we are understanding it is a norm of *recognition*, not reconciliation. Civility identifies requirements that our political advocacy must satisfy if it is to contribute to processes of self-government that are authentically democratic. Civil advocacy achieves this because it is duly attuned to a range of diverse political perspectives that prevail among our equals. Civility sustains the political conditions under which citizens can *look one another in the eye,* so to speak.[14]

The *point* of civility, then, is not deescalation or compromise. Instead, civility identifies a practical stance from which citizens can navigate their political differences democratically. To see this, recall that as we are equals, we each get to exercise our own political judgment. Because political matters are complex, we are not likely to converge on a common set of political opinions. Political difference thus is a direct upshot of our equality. As our political views matter to us, it is natural that we should regard those who hold views that oppose our own as not only wrong, but *in the wrong*. And when it comes to disputes over especially momentous issues, we are bound to see those with whom we disagree as not merely on the *wrong* side of the question, but also on the *unjust* side. A core civic challenge of democratic citizenship is to uphold our commitment to equality while contending with fellow citizens whose political ideas we oppose and may even despise.[15]

Civility—again, in the sense we have developed—provides the standpoint from which this can be done. It enables citizens who are at odds about central political questions to acknowledge one another's equal standing. By embracing the ethos of civility, citizens assure one another of their willingness to behave as fair-dealing democratic partners, despite their severe divisions. In this way, civility is not a recipe for acquiescence or comity. It is a view of properly engaged political advocacy and contestation among democratic equals.

What's more, civility is not centrally concerned with our interpersonal behavior. Rather, it is more a matter of what goes on inside of us when we are engaging in political advocacy. Civility thus is consistent with *real* political disagreement, and thus considerable degrees of rancor and animosity. It does not prescribe soft tones and a polite demeanor, but only seeks to ensure that our political ideas and advocacy are engaged with the views, priorities, and values that our fellow citizens actually hold.

2.3.3.2 Civility and the Imagination

We have seen that the ethos of civility enables us to duly recognize the equal standing of our fellow citizens, despite persistent political differences. In spelling out civility's components I have mentioned that civility does not—indeed, *cannot*—require forms of political activity in which citizens *directly* interact with one another, face-to-face, so to speak. That kind of direct encounter has its value, of course. The point is that civil advocacy can be based in highly indirect modes of engagement, facilitated by various intermediaries like the Press, political parties, citizen associations, and public-interest groups. When functioning properly, these institutions mobilize, collate, and disseminate public political opinion in ways that give citizens access to others' ideas and priorities.

To round out the account, though, it must be emphasized that civility is not simply a matter of acquiring information about others' political viewpoints and giving them adequate consideration. Civility calls for something in addition. In order to advocate in ways that are public-minded, responsive, and transparent, we need not only to learn what our fellow citizens think; we need also to get a sense of *why* they think as they do, what considerations led them to their views. We must not only *take account* of our fellow citizens' perspectives, but also attempt to *get inside* them. Looking our fellow citizens in the eye involves an attempt to see things their way.

Civility thus involves a kind of *perspective-taking*. And given that we cannot directly interact with the vast majority of our fellow citizens, recognizing their equality is partly an *imaginative* endeavor. It calls for a *projection* on our part into their perspective. One form of this kind of projection should be familiar to you. Our democracy is rife with modes of political commentary that ascribe hidden motives, purposes, and objectives to the opposition. Most often, what's ascribed in these contexts is derelict and perverse. We routinely project onto perceived political foes malicious motives and objectives, while tending to cast perceived political allies in a far more favorable light.

Civility of course calls for something different from this more common style of projection. It involves the effort to discern what's underlying others' political views, but in a way that renders our fellow citizens reasonable, legible, and broadly competent. Civil imagination, then, seeks to render our fellow citizens *intelligible*. Crucially, attempting to see our fellow citizens in this light does not require us to moderate our opposition to their views. Although the projection that civility calls for involves a kind of *sympathetic* imagining of others' perspectives, it does not require us to embrace them. Once again, civility is centrally a matter of discerning what views, priorities, and values our fellow citizens actually hold. Thus, civility calls for a mode of imaginative projection that can keep our political disputation and animus well targeted.

2.3.3.3 Civility and the Uncivil

A final matter must be addressed before moving on. I emphasized earlier that responsiveness and transparency do not require citizens to consult with fellow citizens whose views are at odds with the fundamentals of democracy. To repeat, the question of what responsible citizens owe to those who hold antidemocratic political commitments is different from the question we are presently trying to address. As responsiveness and transparency are ingredients of civility, it follows that civility does not invoke a duty for citizens to consult with, listen to, or try to learn from those whose views are beyond the pale.

Yet there remains a question of what responsible citizens owe to those whose views are *not* beyond the pale, but who nevertheless are uncivil—unwilling to conduct political business in a public-minded, responsive, and transparent manner. To be clear, those who espouse political views that are beyond the pale tend also to be uncivil. But not all uncivil citizens are beyond the pale; some are merely *irresponsible* members of the democratic community. They hold views that are consistent with the fundamental commitments of a democratic society, but do not advocate for those ideas in the ways civility requires. They are in this sense not outright opponents of democracy, but noncontributors to the democratic aspiration. We can call them *merely* uncivil. What do we owe to them?

As incivility can take many forms, there could be no general answer to this question. In some cases, engaging civilly with merely uncivil others might be the best practical strategy; their incivility might be due to a lapse or an easily corrected misconception that civil engagement could rectify. In other cases, civil engagement with the merely uncivil might be the best policy simply because it communicates to a broader public one's commitment to civility. However, as civility is an ethos by which we recognize one another's equality in contexts of political disputation, it has a *reciprocal* dimension. It is clear, then, that civility is *not* required of responsible citizens when they are interacting with others who have repeatedly demonstrated a resolute unwillingness to reciprocate. In short, even though responsible citizens do not *owe* civility to those who are merely uncivil, the practical matter of how to engage with the uncivil is too dependent on particular circumstances to be decided here.

In any case, we are trying to formulate a conception of what responsible democratic citizens owe to one another given that they may disagree sharply about crucial matters of politics. Civility thus involves the acknowledgment that disagreement of that kind is *possible* among responsible citizens. In other words, civility is partly a matter of recognizing that citizens who hold political commitments that oppose your own are not thereby beyond the pale and not necessarily uncivil. Indeed, civility provides the standpoint from which we can navigate the fact that there is a broad range of distinct and competing political opinions available to responsible democratic citizens.

2.4 Does Democracy Exist?

We began by identifying democracy with the *ideal* of a self-governing society of equals. Thus, we have been discussing democracy in *ideal* terms. We have not considered how democratic institutions actually function or how citizens really behave toward one another. This way of proceeding occasions a challenge. We all know that material, social, and historical blocks to equal standing among citizens are pervasive in all societies, including those that claim to be democratic. We also know that real-world democratic citizens rarely live up to the civic ethos we have constructed. There is no self-governing society of political equals to be found anywhere on Earth. Does it to follow that democracy doesn't exist, that no society should count as democratic?

Not exactly. To see why, recall that the democratic ideal is an *aspiration*. Earlier, it was claimed that a democracy is a society that *aspires* to be a self-governing society of equals. This means that a society need not *fulfill* the ideal in order to count as democratic. Falling short of the ideal is consistent with being a democracy, provided that the society's institutions and civic practices can plausibly be regarded as striving for the ideal. Given this, certain minimal conditions must be satisfied. For example, no society can plausibly be regarded as even aspiring to the democratic ideal if it does not feature familiar institutions, including routine open elections, a free Press, and codified protections for individual rights. In other words, for a society to count as aspiring to democracy, certain institutions must be in place.

As these are minimal requirements, they're not *sufficient*. What else does it take for a society to plausibly qualify as *aspiring* to democracy? Surely, it's not enough for a leader to *claim* that the regime aims for democracy. Beyond the minimal institutional necessities, what does it take for a society to embrace the democratic aspiration?

We can make progress by asking a question that might seem unrelated. Was Aristotle a scientist? He wrote multiple treatises on scientific subjects, from marine biology and botany to astronomy and physics. Yet he never looked through a microscope and he had no conception of DNA. He also had never heard of the theory of evolution or Newton's laws of motion. Moreover, he affirmed views of natural phenomena that could hardly be called scientific by today's standards. For example, he thought that species were eternal and immutable, the Earth was the center of the universe, that women had fewer teeth than men, and that eels were incapable of procreation. None of these views withstand modern scientific scrutiny. Affirming them today would warrant derision from the scientific community.

Nonetheless, Aristotle sought to explain the world around him by means of a particular style of inquiry, a mode of investigation that directed him to observe, tinker, track changes, theorize in light of the resulting data, and revise as new evidence emerged. He was committed to the enterprise of explanation by means of empirical investigation. For this reason, Aristotle was indeed a scientist. His status as such is due to the aspiration his empirical studies embody, and the way that aspiration guided his work. For the same reason, even though it is reasonable to expect that in a hundred years much of what contemporary scientists believe will be obsolete, they nevertheless are *bona fide* scientists. Being a scientist, then, is not only a matter of holding certain views about the natural world; it also has to do with adopting a certain aim and conducting oneself accordingly.

To take another example, is Taylor Swift an *artist*? Consider the following case that she is not. Restricting ourselves only to musicians, she pales in comparison to the compositional acumen of Mozart or Bach. She also falls short of the virtuosity of Maria Callas, Wes Montgomery, Glenn Gould. Her songwriting skills are not on a par with those of Dolly Parton and Bob Dylan. In what sense is she an artist, then?

One could reasonably dismiss this view as snobbery. But more importantly, the proposed line of reasoning is also mistaken. It is obvious that Taylor Swift is an artist, even though she is not *superlative* along every conceivable dimension of artistic achievement. After all, *no* artist is superlative along all such dimensions. Swift is an artist because she is *driven* by some of the same goals as the mentioned luminaries, and her work embodies some of the same practices. She strives to realize an artistic vision with music; she aspires to a kind of expressive excellence. Her devotion to the *pursuit* of these objectives is what counts.

Indeed, there's an important sense in which *that's* simply what an artist is. Of course, someone who never practices their instrument can't plausibly be said to be aspiring to artistic excellence in music. Similarly, someone who claims to want to write beautiful music but never plays a note and has no understanding of the rudiments of composition is perhaps expressing a sincere *wish* but is not aspiring to be a musician. The crucial point is that embodying the aspiration that makes one a musician is consistent with falling short of the distinctive mode of musical excellence one is striving for. Although being a musician requires that one achieve a certain base level of musical proficiency, what it is to be a musician is to be oriented toward a certain kind of goal. It does not require the realization of that goal, but rather the sincere dedication to its pursuit.

One way to capture this idea is to say that science and art are not defined strictly by their products. They are better understood as *projects*.[16] Once taken up, they orient us toward certain purposes. They thereby also involve adopting the attitudes, habits, and sensibilities that are associated with the effective pursuit of those purposes. We can say, then, that being a scientist or musician is largely a matter of adopting the appropriate ethos. And, beyond achieving baseline competencies, one counts as an artist or a scientist in virtue of being directed by that ethos. In this sense, science and art are both *practices*.[17] They do not require success, or optimal results; one can be a scientist even if one's theory turns out to be false, just as one can be an unsuccessful artist. For similar reasons, wildly guessing the correct answer to a longstanding scientific question does not make one a scientist, nor does one who happens to stumble into a beautiful melody upon first encountering a piano count as a musician.

Something similar holds for democracy. It's the name of a collective political aspiration, a *project* that resides in both the structure of its institutions and the civic practices of its citizens. Accordingly, a society counts as democratic in virtue of the extent to which the aim of achieving a self-governing society of political equals guides its institutions and citizens. This means that a society that falls short of being a self-governing society of political equals might nonetheless qualify as an authentic democracy.

It might seem that this view makes democracy too easy. One might worry that on the proposed account, democracy is simply a matter of *trying*. There's a sense in which someone who puts minimal effort into a project is nonetheless trying to achieve a goal. To address this concern, recall that whether a society is a democracy depends on more than its claim to be one. As noted earlier, certain familiar institutions are required is a society is to count as aspiring to democracy. But that's not all. We have seen that the democratic aspiration also invokes a civic ethos that orients the practices of citizens.

Democracy thus isn't so easy. It is a matter of *us* taking up the democratic project, and therefore embracing the practices of responsible citizenship. Accordingly, even in the presence of stable democratic institutions, our society fails at the democratic aspiration insofar as we are not guided in our political behavior by the ethos of civility. To repeat, democracy depends largely on what goes on inside of us.

Even though no society lives up to the ideal of self-government among equals, democracies can nevertheless exist. Note an important implication. It is common to think of democracy as a form of government that is *founded* or *established*. This leads to the thought that once a democracy is set up, all that remains is the task of keeping it in place. The preceding arguments show that this is an error. Once we understand democracy as an aspiration, we also see that the task of democracy is that of *cultivating* it. Just as the virtuoso musician must continue to develop her technique, citizens must work to enhance and enrich democracy. The democratic aspiration thus involves striving to change it in the direction of greater and more authentic political equality.

2.5 What Democracy Looks Like

What does democracy look like? We can now provide a succinct answer to that question. Insofar as democracy looks like anything at all, it is the image of a society striving to achieve the ideal of a self-government among political equals. This striving is in part a matter of institutions. In order for a society to count as embracing the democratic aspiration, it must uphold certain characteristically democratic institutional arrangements. But those institutions are not sufficient. The democratic aspiration largely resides within the citizens. They must embrace the democratic ethos—the capacities, dispositions, attitudes, and habits that are aimed at realizing the ideal of self-government among equals. This ethos calls citizens to be active participants in democratic politics; but it also requires them to duly recognize the equality of their fellow citizens, even in light of significant political differences. I have identified this ethos as *civility*.

Civility mainly has to do with the ways in which we form, express, adjust, and revise our political judgments. We have seen that in large-scale modern democracies, civility also involves exercises of the imagination, attempts to sympathetically project ourselves into the perspectives of our fellow citizens. Thus, in addition to participation, striving to advance the democratic aspiration calls for citizens to ground their political action in particular forms of political *reflection*. As I have said at several points in our discussion, democracy is thus centrally about what goes on inside of us when we take up our civic role.

It may seem that we have expended a great deal of effort only to arrive at the familiar platitude that a flourishing democracy depends on a citizenry that is both active and reflective. That's the trouble with platitudes—they trick us into thinking that complicated things are simple. The foregoing discussion has provided a rationale for what might be commonplace. This is important because we are now able to see *why* and in *what sense* we must be both active and reflective if we are to meet our civic responsibilities. That's progress.

But there's an additional benefit to having spelled things out in such detail. With the nature of democratic citizenship laid out into component parts, we are better able to track obstacles we might encounter while trying to meet our civic responsibilities. I mentioned earlier that the three components of civility—public-mindedness, responsiveness, and transparency—are mutually reinforcing *in the abstract*. The next chapter will show that *in practice* civility is internally conflicted—its demands push us in opposing directions.

3
Our Polarization Problem

We have been discussing democracy as an aspiration, a kind of society worth striving for. The account has focused on the democratic *ideal*. Yet if we seek to better understand our civic responsibilities, we have to take a look at the current state of democratic politics. It's time to get real.

The scene isn't reassuring. Democracy in the United States is in bad shape. Public trust in central democratic institutions—including Congress and the Supreme Court—is at a historic low.[1] Voters currently report uncommonly high levels of dissatisfaction with elected officials, with young voters in particular expressing intense feelings of political disillusionment.[2] Today's citizens find political discussion across partisan divides "stressful and frustrating."[3] In addition, they are concerned that the current tenor of our politics stokes violence.[4] While voters understandably want politicians to be more cooperative, they also blame only their partisan opponents for political hostility.[5]

Meanwhile, a large proportion of the citizenry remains fixated on debunked conspiracy theories surrounding the 2020 Presidential Election. As of the summer of 2023, a third of the electorate—and two-thirds of Republicans—still claims that widespread voter fraud put Joe Biden in the White House.[6] What's more, the indictments over Donald Trump's efforts to disrupt the transition of power after his election loss seem to have made him only more popular among his followers.[7] As I write this sentence, he is the presumptive presidential nominee for his party in the 2024 election.

These trends have captured the attention of independent democracy watchdogs. In 2017, the Economist Intelligence Unit's

Democracy Index downgraded the United States from a "full democracy" to a "flawed democracy"; the country has since remained in that category.[8] For the past three years, International IDEA has classified the United States as a "backsliding" democracy in its report on the *Global State of Democracy*.[9] While both groups point to the corrosion of democratic institutions and sentiment, they also cite polarization as the primary culprit in the deterioration of US democracy.[10] Indeed, in an interview about the 2021 report, International IDEA's secretary general claimed that the "most concerning" feature of US democracy is "runaway polarization."[11]

This diagnosis will be familiar. Judging from the frequency with which the term "polarization" is used in popular commentary, we can say that it is the "master story" of our democracy's dysfunctions.[12] Pundits from across the spectrum routinely cite polarization as the main ailment of democracy in the United States.[13] The polarization diagnosis is popular among politicians as well. Former Presidents Jimmy Carter and George W. Bush have both recently identified polarization as our society's central challenge, and President Biden has made overcoming polarization and seeking "unity" a core theme.[14] Citizens, too, embrace the ideas that the country is more polarized than ever, that our political divides are expanding, and that politics is dangerously toxic. Oddly, our divided nation agrees that our problem is polarization.

Yet there's less to this consensus than one might think. Popular appeals to polarization tend to be short on details. They don't specify what polarization is and why it's a problem. It is assumed that we all know about polarization. Accordingly, it's easy to get the impression that "polarization" is nothing more than a swanky word used to characterize political divisions that are bitter. We are polarized in this sense simply in virtue of the hostility of our disagreements. Naturally, this popular view of polarization invites the prescription that political rivals must heal their divides, "reach across the aisle," and reconcile.

This chapter argues that polarization indeed poses a considerable threat to democracy. We will find that polarization destabilizes our capacities for civility, thereby undercutting the democratic aspiration. It might seem, then, that the current chapter tells a version of the familiar polarization story. But it doesn't. The account I will develop departs significantly from the common view just sketched. The popular story of polarization can't be *our* story.

Here's why. As was emphasized in the previous chapter, profound political differences are a direct consequence of our equality. Disagreement is a natural byproduct of active, engaged citizenship. Moreover, there is a wide spectrum of opposing political positions that are all compatible with the democratic aspiration. Democratic citizens in good standing thus can differ sharply about politics. And because politics matters, we should expect such divisions to be animated, sometimes even antagonistic. In brief, the popular account of polarization gives political animosity a bad name.

Consider this same point from the other direction. Given the complexity of the issues that citizens must address, widespread political accord should be regarded with suspicion. Enduring political harmony is likely the product either of disengagement or a culture that imposes too high a cost on thinking for oneself.[15] Political hostility thus can be a sign of democracy's health. We therefore should not merely tolerate heated divisions; we should welcome them. The common view of polarization undersells the democratic value of rancor.

So if polarization is indeed the "master story" of democracy's troubles, it must amount to more than the complaint that politics is nasty. In order to be a valuable diagnostic tool, the concept of polarization must enable us to see when our divides are *unduly* deep and *inappropriately* aggressive. Thus, it is not enough to observe that our political divisions are aggravated. In order to determine whether these fractures are democratically pathological, we need to understand what lies under them, what *drives* them. We gain need to look inward, at the attitudes and dispositions that we bring to politics. The popular sense of polarization is too simplistic to be useful here. It must be set aside. To understand the threat that polarization poses, we need a fresh start.

3.1 Getting Our Bearings

When properly formulated, the polarization problem is complex. Our account thus will invoke several philosophical distinctions while drawing on a variety of empirical findings. There is a risk that things will grow unwieldy. To keep ourselves oriented, it will help to call the big picture to mind. Let's take a moment to get our bearings.

We are building an argument for the thesis that responsible citizenship calls for civic solitude, occasions for a distinctive kind of reflective activity that can be engaged only in isolation from one's fellow citizens. The preceding chapter took the first step by developing a view of responsible democratic citizenship. We will now identify a difficulty at the heart of that office, a pathology that emerges out of our earnest efforts to meet our civic responsibilities.

To get the flavor of this difficulty, recall our account of civility. It says that citizens must be politically active and respectful of the equality of their fellow citizens. To do this, citizens must advocate in ways that are public-minded, responsive, and transparent. We saw that in addition to familiar forms of public action and engagement, civility also calls for exercises of political imagination, attempts to see things from others' points of view. In short, responsible citizenship involves characteristic forms of political activity as well as distinctive modes of political reflection.

Now for the trouble. Empirical results suggest that our civic responsibilities tend to work at cross purposes. Characteristically democratic political action can undo our capacities for democratic reflection. In taking responsibility for our democracy, we subvert our ability to satisfy our responsibilities to our fellow citizens. In striving to live up to some of the requirements for responsible citizenship, we undercut others. Democratic citizenship is *morally conflicted*.

We will see that this conflict is due to the *polarization dynamic*. It has the effect of rendering partisan affiliation our primary way of understanding ourselves and our relations to others. With partisan identity at the center of all that we do, we grow increasingly inclined to regard our fellow citizens as either political accomplices or impediments, not equals. In the end, the polarization dynamic fosters the attitude that civility is owed only to those who share our politics. That's a profoundly antidemocratic stance.

Still, the polarization dynamic has its source in vital democratic activity, modes of political engagement that are necessary for democracy to thrive. Thus, the problem of polarization resides *within* the office of citizenship. It therefore cannot be eliminated, but only mitigated. It's not too far-fetched to say, then, that democracy is subject to an *autoimmune disorder*.

The task of this chapter is straightforward. It explains the polarization dynamic and the pathologies it provokes. The result will be that in addition to civil modes of political advocacy, responsible citizenship requires us to take steps to moderate the impact of the polarization dynamic. Democratic citizenship thus is partly a *management* task.

However, given the internal source of the dynamic, managing polarization calls for us to do something *different from* the usual. Our conception of the responsibilities of citizenship must be expanded. This result lays the foundation for Chapter 4, which argues that civic solitude is required if we are to decenter our partisan selves and manage polarization.

That's the roadmap. The first item on our agenda is to explain what polarization is. As noted above, we need to begin by untangling the word.

3.2 Two Kinds of Polarization

We can start by distinguishing two phenomena that are called polarization: *political* polarization and *belief* polarization.[16] Once these are understood independently, we will examine their interaction. This will allow us to locate the problem of polarization within the cumulative impact of political and belief polarization working in concert—the polarization dynamic.

Here's the rough distinction. Political polarization has to do with the *ideological divide* between political groups. To keep things simple, we can talk about political parties, even though political polarization can beset political formations of other kinds—associations, alliances, constituencies, communities, and so on. Political polarization resides in the relation between political parties. It is a *sociological* condition having to do with specifically *political* units.

By contrast, belief polarization is a *cognitive* phenomenon that occurs within likeminded groups, whether they're political or not. It is the tendency for people to transform into more extreme versions of themselves as a result of interactions with their peers. Although belief polarization triggers a negative stance toward an out-group, it is not fundamentally a *relation* between opposing groups. Rather, it has to do with tendencies *within* an alliance. It is a shift that occurs among allies.

In a nutshell, then, political polarization measures the divide between political parties, while belief polarization is a cognitive shift toward extremity that occurs within likeminded groups, whether they are political or not. Such are the broad strokes. Let's turn to the details.

3.2.1 Political Polarization

We have already said that political polarization is a metric of the *ideological distance* between rival political parties. When it is pronounced, the common ground among the parties falls away, thereby leaving little basis for cooperation and compromise. This kind of polarization thus results in political deadlock and frustration. This can be debilitating in legislative contexts. If democracy is to flourish, government must be able to get things done, after all. Intense political polarization typically results in governmental stalemate and paralysis.

The phenomenon of political polarization is straightforward and, I suspect, sadly familiar. Yet the notion of "ideological distance" remains vague. What does it mean for two parties to be ideologically distant?

We can distinguish three ways of construing this distance. It can be gauged in terms of party platforms, purity among party elites, or cross-partisan animosity among ordinary citizens. Sometimes these are treated as competing interpretations of political polarization. There hence is an ongoing debate among researchers concerning which measure ideological distance is optimal.[17] That debate can be sidestepped here. We can treat the three measures as distinct sites where the relevant fractures emerge.

3.2.1.1 Three Sites of Political Polarization

One construal of ideological distance focuses on the official doctrines of the opposed groups. When looking at political parties, we examine their platforms. Two parties are politically polarized to the degree that their official political agendas are opposed, feature no common objectives, or are in some other sense contrary to each other. Refer to this species of political polarization as *platform* polarization.

A second way of measuring ideological distance looks at party leaders, officials, and high-profile affiliates. It determines the extent of unanimity within the party. Opposed groups are highly polarized in this sense when their membership includes very few moderates or bridge-builders. As it focuses on party elites, call this *elite* polarization.

Elite polarization involves the shunning of moderates. In the United States, it is reflected in the disappearance of "liberal conservatives" and "conservative liberals" from the two major parties.[18] Elite polarization typically is accompanied by the stance that cooperation with the other side is a kind of betrayal. When elite polarization is dominant, political groups valorize purity. And as purity becomes central to the party's collective identity, moderates are sidelined, and the hardliners take control.

But the thing about hardliners is that they feel the need to *prove* their commitment to the group's ideals. They tend to do this in two related ways. First, they escalate their expressions of contempt for the opposition; second, they call out other members of the group as insincere, inauthentic, or twofaced. Accordingly, as expressions of contempt for the opposition escalate, a vernacular for ridiculing moderates within the group also develops.[19] The result is political deadlock accompanied by intensifying in-group and cross-partisan animosity among elites.

There is room for debate over the extent to which the United States is currently polarized in the two ways just mentioned.[20] But there is no such ground for dispute with respect to our third way of understanding ideological distance. By all accounts, the United States currently is in the grip of severe *affective* polarization.[21] Unlike platform and elite polarization, which are both focused on the major parties, affective polarization looks toward ordinary citizens. It gauges ideological distance by examining the attitudes of rank-and-file party affiliates, ordinary people who identify with one of the major parties.[22]

Affective polarization is a condition where citizens embrace intensely negative attitudes and dispositions toward those perceived to be politically dissimilar from themselves, and correspondingly warm feelings toward perceived allies.[23] Two political parties are affectively polarized to the extent that their ordinary affiliates dislike those who embrace an opposing political identity. Note here that regardless of whether affective polarization is *symmetrical* across partisan divides, we should expect it to escalate *reciprocally*.[24] That is, as one side amplifies its animus against its opposition, the other side is likely to intensify its negative stance, too.

As affective polarization fixes on the attitudes that ordinary citizens take toward their perceived opponents and allies, it need not track actual policy disputes.[25] Citizens are affectively polarized simply in virtue of the animosity they harbor for their political adversaries. This feature of the phenomenon is important because although affective polarization has escalated drastically over the past four decades in the United States, citizens' differences over key policies have either remained stable or eased.[26]

What's more, citizens do not only report high levels of mere *dislike* for affiliates of the opposing party. They also see them as untrustworthy, ignorant, threatening, dangerous, and divested from democracy. Affective polarization thus amounts to more than *antipathy* for the other side; it manifests as *animosity* for them. Consider that according to one recent study, 60 percent of Republicans and 62 percent of Democrats see the other party as a "serious threat" to the United States, while roughly 40 percent of people in both parties describe the opposing party as "downright evil."[27] Other data show that 15 percent of Republicans and 20 percent of Democrats claim that our democracy would be healthier if a large number of their political opponents "just died."[28]

That is to say, when affective polarization is pronounced, cross-partisan animosity is *localized*. It targets *fellow citizens*, not only the opposing side's politicians and leaders.[29] And that's not all. Affective polarization in the United States is also *personalized*. In addition to rejecting perceived rivals' politics, citizens also despise the opposing side *as people*. They begin to loath the overall behavior of their partisan opposition. The clothes they wear, the vehicles they drive, the food they eat, their modes of entertainment, and much else have become sites of ridicule.[30] Given this, it is perhaps unsurprising that in the United States popular disapproval of interpartisan marriage is now more pronounced than disapproval of inter-faith and inter-racial marriage.[31] Parents in the United States would rather see their child marry someone who worships a false God than votes for the wrong candidate!

Perhaps this is not so outlandish as it may seem. After all, in the United States, co-partisanship is the most reliable predictor of romantic compatibility.[32] However, this trend suggests more than a prudent strategy for healthy intimate relations. Our partisan affinities go far deeper. We find faces more appealing when they are presented alongside cues that suggest favorable partisanship; we find the very same faces less attractive when presented alongside indicators of political affiliation that opposes our own.[33] That is, quite apart from dating preferences, we find those who share our politics more physically attractive. Our partisan affiliation informs our perceptions of other people, reaching down all the way into our assessment of their physical attributes.

As I mentioned, affective polarization in the United States has intensified drastically even though policy divisions have remained stable. Yet citizens nonetheless *believe* that their policy disagreements are especially deep and intensifying.[34] They think that partisan differences over specific political issues are wider than ever. More specifically, they believe that while their own party's positions have not changed very much, the policy agenda of the opposition has become drastically more radical. As one would expect, citizens also attribute sharply opposing—and militant—values to their rivals. They moreover regard their own political group as the target of intense negative attitudes from the opposing side. That is, affective polarization invokes a kind of partisan persecution complex; we come to see our partisan rivals as out to get us.[35] We regard them not only as politically misguided, but as social and personal threats.

These projections are generally inaccurate.[36] Affective polarization thus gives rise to a "perception gap" among partisan citizens.[37] When affective polarization is pronounced, we systematically misconstrue the ideas, values, and dispositions of our partisan opponents. We see them as far more extreme, ruthless, militant, aggressive, and threatening than they are. We thus become more susceptible to misinformation that affirms our partisan prejudices.[38] We hence naturally seek to disassociate from them. This in turn amplifies our biases against them.[39]

A plausible account of this mismatch is that citizens discover that they hold their partisan opposition in contempt, and then *infer* that their opponents embrace radically opposed political views.[40] In other words, we discover our cross-partisan animosity and then seek to *rationalize* it. The intense negative affect toward the opposition comes first, and then citizens explain their contempt by projecting on to the opposition fundamentally dissimilar values, commitments, and objectives. Citizens over-ascribe obnoxious positions to their partisan rivals as a way of making sense of their animosity toward them. Crucially, these misattributions are most prevalent among citizens who report high levels of political information and engagement.[41] Insofar as these partisans set the tone for their more causal affiliates, citizens become engrossed with their party's unflattering portrayals of the other side.

3.2.1.2 The Three Sites as Mutually Reinforcing

We have been exploring different ways in which one might gauge the "ideological distance" between opposed political parties. Although these three ways of thinking about ideological distance are independent of one another, it is illuminating to consider how they might interact. Specifically, heightened levels of affective polarization can help explain the pervasiveness of elite and platform polarization.[42]

First, consider that when citizens intensely dislike those outside of their own partisan tribe, elite polarization is incentivized. After all, politicians seek to win elections. And it's increasingly the case in the United States that elections at the state and national levels are won mainly by way of partisan mobilization. Although it's advisable for candidates to court new voters, their most reliable path to electoral victory has to do with provoking political behavior from their base.[43] It is well documented that animosity, distrust, resentment, and contempt are potent behavioral triggers.[44] Indeed, citizens who manifest high levels of cross-party animosity are more likely than their mild-mannered co-partisans to vote.[45] So when citizens harbor intense negative affect for the other side, candidates and party leaders do well to amplify their hostility toward the opposing party.

This in turn incentivizes platform polarization. When expressing hostility for the other side is a winning political strategy for candidates, the parties naturally follow suit. They are incentivized to exhibit a wholesale repudiation of the other side's agenda, to embrace a platform that negates that of the opposition. Widespread affective polarization hence makes for easy campaigning. Candidates are well advised to demonize the opposition, valorize intransigence, and stoke animosity among the base. They can do this by pledging to obstruct, oppose, and undo whatever the other party stands for. None of these strategic maneuvers requires candidates to design a positive policy agenda of their own. This in turn feeds back to citizens, fueling negative affect toward partisan rivals, and thereby accelerating affective polarization. In short, regardless of how overall levels of platform, elite, and affective polarization may differ in the United States, the three sites of political polarization are mutually reinforcing.

I suspect the alarming circumstances associated with political polarization are familiar. Yet they are also curious. The fact that affective polarization has escalated so drastically in the absence of similar intensifications of policy differences is puzzling. It calls for explanation. Hence our next question is why affective polarization is so widespread. To unravel this puzzle, we need to look at the phenomenon of belief polarization.

3.2.2 Belief Polarization

Recall that belief polarization is a cognitive shift that occurs within likeminded groups.[46] It is a phenomenon where our interactions with likeminded others transform us into more extreme versions of ourselves. In this way, it is similar to what is popularly called the "yes man" phenomenon. However, belief polarization shows that when we surround ourselves with "yes men," we not only tend to grow more convinced of the correctness of our ideas; we also adopt exaggerated formulations of them.

A quick sketch of some of the experimental findings will illustrate the basic tendency. In the earliest studies, a group of French students holding positive views of Charles De Gaulle and negative views of American foreign policy came to adopt even more positive views of De Gaulle and increasingly intense negative assessments of American foreign policy in the course of group discussion.[47] In another experiment around the same time, American high schoolers who were already disposed to racial prejudice came to hold more severely prejudiced views in the wake of discussion with a likeminded group about racism in America; meanwhile, students in the same school who embraced low level of racial prejudice emerged from discussion with likeminded others with even lower levels of prejudice.[48] Similar studies have shown that discussion of sexism within groups of feminists leads participants to adopt more radically feminist commitments, while discussion of the same topics among chauvinists leads to an escalation of chauvinistic sentiment.[49]

A more recent finding has it that broadly liberal citizens come to adopt more stridently liberal views after interactions with other liberal citizens; conservative citizens become more resolutely conservative as a result of likeminded encounters as well.[50] That is, in belief polarization, liberals become *more* liberal, and conservatives become *more* conservative. These latter findings demonstrate that belief polarization impacts more than individual *beliefs*. It also intensifies one's commitment to one's overall perspective.

Belief polarization applies to groups of all kinds. It is not restricted to those that are allied on political or moral issues. For example, when people who agree that a given chair is especially comfortable get together to discuss the merits of the chair, each person increases their assessment of the chair's coziness.[51] Those who find a particular celebrity especially attractive emerge from group discussion holding that the celebrity is even more appealing than they initially thought.[52] Belief polarization also has been observed also where groups are likeminded with respect to trivial matters of fact. When people who agree that the city of Denver, Colorado, is notable for its elevation discuss the matter, they each come to believe that Denver is *higher* than they originally supposed.[53]

This survey barely scratches the surface of the empirical documentation of belief polarization.[54] It is safe to say that the phenomenon is remarkably common.[55] It has been studied for more than six decades and found within likeminded groups of all kinds. We already have seen that it does not discriminate between different types of belief: likeminded groups polarize over ordinary matters of fact, judgments of personal taste, and deep questions about value. Moreover, the phenomenon operates regardless of the *point* of the group's interaction. They polarize when they are deciding what the group will do, but also when their interaction has no particular objective. Finally, belief polarization does not vary with nationality, race, gender, religion, economic status, or level of education.

We will discuss the mechanism by which belief polarization operates in a moment. For now, note that the phenomenon involves a change in our grasp of the basis of our beliefs. As we surround ourselves with others who affirm our opinions, we come to overstate the weight of the supporting evidence for our shared commitment.[56] We thereby also become more dogmatic, increasingly unreceptive to counterevidence and resistant to correction.

Unsurprisingly, we also grow more inclined to dismiss detractors as irrational, uninformed, and benighted.[57] We become less inclined to listen to them, and more prone to interrupt when they're speaking.[58] And as our *confidence* escalates, we opt for more exaggerated and strident formulations of the opinions we share in common with our allies.

Belief polarization thus involves two shifts in our beliefs. Likeminded interaction leads us to adopt more *extreme* versions of our beliefs. But it also escalates our *confidence*. To employ some terminology from academic philosophy, belief polarization extremifies the *content* of our beliefs while also escalating our *degree* of belief. So, we adopt a more extreme belief, and we also hold that new belief with greater confidence than that with which we held its ancestor.

Yet belief polarization is not only about individuals and their beliefs. Remember that it is a *group dynamic*. Its effects go beyond shifting individuals toward more extreme opinions and greater confidence. In belief polarization, the *group* also becomes more extreme and confident. This is because group members fuel one another's escalation; they egg each other on. And as groups shift toward extremity, the members also become more aware of their bond with the other members. They *see themselves* as allies. This leads them to be more disposed to act in concert, to behave *as a group*. And, again, as the shift escalates *confidence*, the group grows more inclined to engage in risky behavior on behalf of their extremified commitment.[59]

To put this in a nutshell, we can say that belief polarization provokes extremity along a few different dimensions. In the course of engaging with likeminded others, we come to adopt beliefs that are more strident than the ones we held before the interaction. Moreover, we come to hold these new beliefs with an escalated degree of conviction. But we also experience an uptick in confidence in *ourselves*; we grow more assured of the correctness of our overall perspective. We thus come to more deeply identify with others who share that perspective. And as a result, we also grow less risk averse when it comes to collective action with our allies.

Yet this is not the entirety of the phenomenon. As groups shift in these ways, members are also incentivized to withhold information and hide preferences that deviate from the group's customs and expectations.[60] Accordingly, belief polarized groups tend also to become *more alike* in ways that go beyond their initial shared opinions.[61] As they come to see themselves as allies, they devise ways of signaling to one another their shared commitment to the group. In other words, as they become more alike, they also become more invested in being alike—and, crucially, in *remaining* alike. Our more extreme selves are also more conformist. Belief polarization *homogenizes* likeminded coalitions, it makes members more *groupish*.

The tendency toward homogenization is not difficult to explain. Belief polarization intensifies negative assessments of outsiders. As we become more extreme, so too does our negative affect towards an out-group. This gives rise to strong social boundaries, which in turn lead the members of belief polarized groups to fixate on the *differences* between insiders and outsiders. Needing to establish sharp lines separating favored allies and dreaded foes, belief polarized groups come to adopt increasingly exacting standards for authentic membership.

But to do their job, these standards must be public—they must be *visible* markers of membership. Indicators of authenticity thus come to encompass behaviors and attitudes that extend beyond the group's defining ideas.[62] Consequently, membership expands into a matter of adopting the group's "worldview" or *lifestyle*—including its prevalent habits, slogans, gestures, and characteristic attire.[63] Compliance with these broader expectations *expresses* one's membership and group loyalty. As public qualifications for good-standing membership intensify, the group develops means for detecting poseurs. As such, belief polarized groups also tend to exhibit the Black Sheep Effect—their negative attitudes towards phony allies are more intense than those they take towards outright enemies.[64]

Further, as groups become more overtly conformist, they also become more reliant on centralized standard-setters to establish the indicators of genuine membership. Enforcement mechanisms hence also emerge, ways of compelling the desired behaviors and disciplining deviations. In this way, belief polarization renders groups more hierarchical and therefore less internally democratic. As conformity pressure intensifies, even slight divergences from the group's expectations are amplified into serious infractions. Belief polarized groups thus tend to shrink into smaller cohorts of hardliners.

It should be repeated once more that belief polarization is a *cognitive* phenomenon that occurs with *group* interactions. Although it is reliably prompted when likeminded individuals share their ideas and perspectives, belief polarization is not fundamentally driven by information. We will see shortly that belief polarization occurs regardless of whether likeminded interaction discloses new evidence that favors the group's shared viewpoint. In this sense, belief polarization is not necessarily a *reason-tracking* process; groups can shift into extremity independently of any justification for doing so. Although it changes our beliefs and escalates our confidence, the phenomenon itself has more to do with the desire to fit in.

3.2.2.1 How Belief Polarization Works

Belief polarization is so common that one wonders how it works. Two intuitive accounts of belief polarization's mechanism leap to mind—call them the *Information View* and the *Comparison View*. Each has its virtues, but neither can be the full story about how belief polarization occurs. We'll consider them briefly before exploring a better option.

The Information View holds that belief polarization results from the *informational filters* that operate within likeminded groups. Parties to likeminded interactions tend to share information that supports the group's stance. As a consequence, group members hear many confirming voices. And insofar as countervailing considerations are mentioned at all, they are given short shrift. Group members thus develop a skewed sense of the relevant evidence. It begins to see to them that a *more strident* version of their initial belief is warranted. And given that counterbalancing information has been suppressed or dismissed, they come to view their new commitment as all the more obviously correct. Accordingly, they adopt an elevated degree of confidence.

The Information View is undeniably intuitive. Indeed, informational filters are reliable instruments by which belief polarization can be initiated. Yet the Information View is not correct. This is because belief polarization has been found even when discussion partners share no information in support of their shared commitment. In other words, "mere exposure" to a likeminded group—interactions that involve no exchange of information favoring the group's commitment—is enough to set the phenomenon in motion.[65]

This points to a second intuitive account of belief polarization's mechanism, the Comparison View. It contends that belief polarization occurs because group members strive to be seen by peers as *authentic* advocates of the group's commitment. Wishing to appear to their allies as "desirably distinctive," subjects adjust their belief and confidence to be slightly above what they perceive to be the group mean.[66] They try to outdo other members in their expressions of commitment. As the individuals who compose the group are simultaneously recalibrating in this way, something like an authenticity arms race develops, leading the group as a whole to shift toward greater extremity and confidence.

The Comparison View certainly has its advantages over the Information View. For one thing, it recognizes that belief polarization is not necessarily a reason-tracking process. It correctly treats belief polarization as a *group* dynamic. Nonetheless, the

Comparison View falters. Although in-group social comparison is a reliable way of *initiating* belief polarization, it is not necessary for the phenomenon. Belief polarization can beset likeminded groups even when their interactions provide no basis for the kind of interpersonal calibration that the Comparison View requires.[67]

A better account of belief polarization's mechanism is the *Corroboration View*. It holds that belief polarization is driven by group-affiliated *validation* of one's perspective. Put roughly, it says that we shift into our more extreme selves when we feel that a group with which we identify affirms the same beliefs and attitudes that we espouse. According to the Corroboration View, then, we need not hear new evidence, nor need we compare ourselves to our peers. Instead, we extremify simply in light of the realization that a view we hold is *popular* among our identity group. We shift into our more extreme, confident, and committed selves because it *feels good* to fit in with those who we consider peers.

The Corroboration View hence treats belief polarization as centrally a matter of affect and group affinity, rather than information or social comparisons. Nonetheless, it can explain why likeminded information exchange and in-group comparisons reliably instigate belief polarization. After all, these are both ways of situating oneself within a peer group and garnering its affirmation. Hence the Corroboration View need not deny that the other accounts capture paths by which belief polarization emerges. It holds simply that the mechanism driving the phenomenon has to do with the positive affect that results when we receive validation from our peers.

Consequently, the Corroboration View is supported by the results that are cited in favor of the other two views. But it can also explain additional features of belief polarization that are less easily accommodated by the Information and Comparison accounts. For example, research shows that extremity shifts are more severe when group membership is primed and significantly less pronounced when interaction occurs among likeminded subjects who do not regard themselves as sharing a group identity.[68] This is precisely what the Corroboration View predicts. Moreover, experimenters have found that extremity shifts do not vary significantly with the composition of the group; in other words, groups that contain a few extreme members do not shift more radically than groups composed entirely of moderates.[69] The Corroboration View accommodates this finding nicely. It holds simply that corroboration from our peers makes us *feel* good about our beliefs, and this affirmation of our self-ascribed identity leads us to shift toward extremity; this affective boost can occur regardless of whether the group members are themselves extreme or moderate.[70]

Consider one more feature of belief polarization that speaks in favor of the Corroboration View. It turns out that belief polarization can be activated by way of highly indirect channels. For example, presenting a liberal subject with a chart showing that liberals widely oppose genetically modified food can prompt belief polarization. Similarly, exposure to a poll showing that conservatives strongly favor a particular military intervention can produce an extremity shift in a conservative who already favors that action.[71] What's more, the relevant environmental prompts need not be verbal, overt, or literal. They can be merely implicit signals to group members that some belief is prevalent among them. Hats, pins, campaign signs, logos, gestures, songs, emblems, and the like—roughly any environmental feature that makes salient a group identity and the attitudes that are popular within it—can initiate belief polarization among those who share that identity.[72]

Again, these results are consistent with the Corroboration View. It says that what matters for belief polarization is validation from a peer group with which one identifies. Hence there is no reason why the relevant affirmation must come directly from the peers in the flesh, so to speak. The Corroboration View recognizes that although interpersonal interaction is a reliable setting for belief polarization, it is not strictly necessary.

3.2.2.2 Belief Polarization and the Stadium

We have seen that belief polarization fundamentally has to do with triggers of group identity. We extremify in response to the affirmation of a group with which we identify. To get a better handle on how this happens, let's consider what might initially seem a far-fetched analogy.

If you're a fan of a particular sports team, think of the last time you were in a stadium packed with your fellow fans watching your team take the lead a championship match. Chances are that you showed up dressed in a way that signals your team allegiance. You might have worn an official jersey, or else dressed in the team's colors. Of course, more extreme signals of team-affiliation—face painting, dying one's hair, wearing elaborate costumes, and so on—are not uncommon. But in addition to this, you likely shared special phrases or slogans, gestures, and chants with other fans, as ways to expressing to them your dedication. What's more, during the play, you probably acted in concert with the other fans—standing, cheering, and singing together. As your team began to take the lead, your overall enthusiasm swelled. In the midst of all the excitement, your commitment to the team intensified—you became *more* of a fan. You escalated your sense of the team's merit, and perhaps even began to take pride in their excellence. Meanwhile, your negative estimation of the opposing team and its fans also escalated. You might have come to see them as pitiful or repulsive. In the case of a longstanding team rivalry, it's likely that your side began taunting, belittling, or provoking the fans of the other team.

Take stock of how many of these attitudes and dispositions persist outside of the stadium on gameday. Again, if you are a sports fan, it is not unlikely that you decorate your home, car, and workspace with team merchandise and memorabilia. You probably seek to express your commitment even in the offseason. What's more, you probably know someone who couldn't bear the thought of wearing a rival team's jersey, or even of befriending one of their fans. Personal rifts among fans of rival teams are common enough to be the stuff of popular comedy.

Now here's the point. Fandom structures social interaction outside of the stadium, erecting barriers to certain encounters while encouraging others. Observe further that in many cases, fandom is bound up with broad features of one's lifestyle. Corporations that produce consumer goods frequently partner with sports teams. Accordingly, products ranging from cars and televisions to footwear, alcohol, and snacks are marketed on the basis of team identification. Merchandise that may otherwise be unrelated to sports is *branded* as especially for the fans of a particular team. Being an authentic fan of a particular team hence is bound up with priorities, preferences, and habits that extend into the whole of life. Fans of the same team thus tend to share a good deal more in common than their team loyalty. Fandom *consolidates* life around the team.

Now, if sports are not your thing, a similar illustration can be given of large-scale group encounters of various other kinds. Again, belief polarization occurs when a common social identity to be made salient to a group of people, and then affirmed. Think of rock concerts. Like the sports fans, attendees typically dress alike and engage in behaviors designed to signal their fandom to other fans. What's more, performers are well advised to incorporate audience participation into their shows. By prompting the fans to sing together, engage in call-and-response routines, and gesture in similar ways, the performer primes them to see themselves as a group. Fans thereby come to feel more invested in that common identity, and thus more devoted to the performer. In the course of the collective encounter, their positive attitudes are elevated. This is why seeing your favorite band perform live typically makes you a bigger fan. The same goes for megachurch worship services, corporate retreats, and, of course, political rallies.

The Corroboration View holds that belief polarization works roughly like fandom. It is activated when a favored group identity is made salient, and one is made to feel *authenticated* by the group.

This affirmation brings with it elevated affect that seeks additional validation. We can say, then, that in addition to extremification and homogenization, belief polarization involves the *centering* of a primed social identity. It emerges from peer authentication, and then *reinforces* our identification with them. Accordingly, as we belief polarize, we more *fully* identify with our peers. Thus we grow more invested in maintaining the borders between the in-group and the out-group. This leads to an escalation of efforts to police that border, and thus to the introduction of an expanding set of standards for authentic group membership. But, as we have noted previously, when a group becomes fixated on sustaining clear boundaries between the insiders and outsiders, it grows more reliant on centralized standard-setters to establish the broadening criteria for authenticity.

To repeat, belief polarization *consolidates* one's life around group membership. It *centers* a group identity, transforming it into the predominant lens through which one understands a broad range of other aspects of social life, including interpersonal relationships. And, as was also mentioned earlier, as likeminded groups become more alike, they become more committed to staying alike. They thus grow more conformist and more negatively disposed to outsiders. This leads them to fixate on the boundaries between the in-group and the out-group. Accordingly, belief polarization leads us to see the entire social world as structured by or group affiliations and rivalries.

Perhaps all of this sounds vaguely familiar? If so, that's understandable. If you attended high school in the United States, the description of belief polarization should have prompted memories of your teenage years. Belief polarization is fundamentally a clique phenomenon.

3.2.3 A Review

We have surveyed a lot of material quickly, so let's pause for a moment to review. We distinguished political polarization from belief polarization. You will recall that political polarization measures the ideological distance between political parties. "Ideological distance" can be understood in at least three different ways. Our discussion of political polarization focused largely on what is called *affective* polarization, which mainly has to do with the negative emotions and dispositions that rank-and-file citizens present toward perceived political opponents. We then saw that pronounced levels of affective polarization reinforce tendencies to intensify divides among party elites and the platforms of political parties. The three sites of political polarization thus reinforce one another.

Our discussion of political polarization uncovered a puzzle. Affective polarization has intensified in the absence of a corresponding increase in the divisions among citizens over public policy. We despise those on the other side more intensely than ever, while the actual depth of our policy differences has generally remained steady over the past forty years. What could explain this?

To get traction on this puzzle, we turned to belief polarization, a cognitive phenomenon that occurs within likeminded groups. Roughly, it involves two related shifts among allies: extremification and homogenization. As likeminded people interact, they become more extreme in their ideas, more confident in their perspective, and also more conformist. All of this can occur in the absence of new information or evidence that would warrant these shifts. Crucially, as members of a coalition become more confident and more similar to their allies, they also grow increasingly hostile toward perceived outsiders. In this sense, escalating negative affect toward an out-group is part of the belief polarization phenomenon. More importantly, as belief polarization is not a reason-tracking phenomenon, it can prompt escalations of negative affect for an out-group independently of our actual differences with them.

However, this connection between belief polarization and escalating negative affect is not sufficient to resolve our puzzle. Recall that affective polarization is tied specifically to *partisan* groups, while belief polarization occurs within likeminded groups of any kind. To address the puzzle of why affective polarization has skyrocketed in the absence of correspondingly expanding policy differences, we need an account of why specifically *partisan* animosity has accelerated.

The Corroboration View of belief polarization helps solidify the connection between belief polarization and affective polarization. Remember that according to the Corroboration View, extremification and homogenization result from the affective boost we feel when a peer group with which we identify *affirms* and *authenticates* our point of view. Belief polarization hence involves the *centering* of a group identity. As we extremify, we come more fully to *identify* with a group, we come to see ourselves through the lens of membership. We thus also internalize the group's negative attitudes and dispositions toward outsiders.

This begins to address to our puzzle. When our *political units* are heavily belief polarized, our partisan identities are centered. Under these conditions, we should expect affective polarization to intensify independently of actual policy differences. Thus, a hypothesis: the reason why affective polarization has drastically escalated in the absence of similarly intensified differences over policy is that our political coalitions have become significantly belief polarized. The next section develops a case for this hypothesis.

3.3 Centering the Partisan Self: Sorting and Saturation

One measure of belief polarization within a group is the extent to which the collective identity is centered among its members. We can gauge this by looking at the degree to which the identity has permeated the members' social worlds, the role that membership plays in seemingly diffuse aspects of their lives. Where a specific group identity is central, we should expect it to correlate with a broad range of lifestyle features, including preferred patterns of social interaction.

By this standard, partisan identity is thoroughly centered in the United States today. Political affiliation is increasingly the primary way in which we position ourselves socially.[73] It is currently our most durable form of social self-identification, now occupying the situating roles that religious, ethnic, and racial affiliations once played in society. Moreover, partisan affiliation is now tightly correlated with these other sites of social identity; that is, racial, ethnic, and religious affiliations are tightly aligned with political identity.[74] In the United States, once citizens adopt a partisan affiliation, they more commonly change religious affiliation than partisan loyalty.[75]

We can understand how this has come about by considering the phenomena of *partisan sorting* and *political saturation*.[76] Start with the former. Over the past several decades, the United States has grown more socially diverse in various encouraging respects. Meanwhile, however, the local spaces that citizens inhabit in their daily lives have become more politically homogeneous.[77]

Look at the household. Families in the United States are now substantially more politically uniform than they were thirty years ago.[78] Liberals and conservatives also exhibit distinct parenting styles that reflect their systematically different views about what makes for a good child.[79] They also give their children different types of names.[80] Moreover, partisan rivals live in different kinds of homes; conservatives get married at a younger age and have more children than liberals, so their houses tend to be larger.[81] They also reside in distinct kinds of neighborhood. Liberals like densely populated areas with sidewalks, while conservatives favor communities with fewer sidewalks and larger yards.[82] Even large cities have liberal and conservative districts.[83]

These trends extend well beyond the domestic sphere. Schools, workplaces, occupations, and religious congregations exhibit these same patterns. They, too, tend to be tightly segregated along partisan lines.[84] Liberals and conservatives send their children to different schools, work different kinds of jobs, and attend different religious services. As a result, they live in spatially distinct social environments. These spatial divides naturally impact their personal habits. Liberals and conservative dress differently, express dissimilar aesthetic preferences, and even exhibit distinct patterns of speech.[85] They feed their pets different kinds of food, take different kinds of vacation, and enjoy different forms of recreation.[86] Additionally, they watch different television programs and seek out different kinds of entertainment.[87] In the United States today, consumer preferences across the board—from beer and coffee to movies, cars, clothing, and vacations—strongly correlate with partisan identity.[88] It is no stretch to say that our lives are consolidated around our partisan divide. And as a result, politics is largely a matter of branding.

I'm sure that these patterns are so evident that I do not need to spell out the specifics. You can anticipate them perfectly well. Liberals watch art films, enjoy Starbucks coffee and microbrews, drive hybrid cars, vacation in foreign countries, wear yoga pants, and transport organic groceries bought at Whole Foods in reusable tote bags. Meanwhile, conservatives drive pickup trucks and SUVs, drink Coors beer and Dunkin' coffee, eat at Cracker Barrel, watch network TV, dress in camouflage, and vacation in domestic locations that offer opportunities for fishing and hunting. It is important to note that these familiar trends hold steady across geographical and economic differences.[89] Rich conservatives in Georgia tend to have more in common with their poorer copartisans in Iowa than they share with economically similar liberal Georgians.

And so we arrive once again at the point that partisan affiliation functions in the United States more as a *lifestyle* than a stance about policy or the role of government. Indeed, the policy commitments that ordinary citizens express tend to be driven by their partisan affiliation, not the other way around. Partisan affiliation comes first, and citizens formulate their policy opinions to fit the party line.[90] This is why in experimental settings, subjects who oppose a policy proposal when it is presented as preferred by their partisan opponents will support that same policy when it is described as favored by their party.[91] Again, democracy in the United States is about identity, not government.

Social sorting is an unsurprising phenomenon. It is also inevitable. Humans are social creatures, and we feel most at home among others who are like us. *Homophily*—the tendency to seek company with those who are similar to us—comes naturally. Accordingly, social sorting is no problem as such. The trouble lies in the fact that social sorting now occurs nearly exclusively around a *single* kind of social categorization, namely political affiliation.

Forty years ago, social spaces in the United States were sorted according to a range of distinct affiliations—religion, race, ethnicity, culture, class, and so on. Religious services would typically bring together people from different walks of life; co-workers in the same office commonly shared little else than an employer; and neighborhoods organized around a common ethnic or cultural identity tended to be economically diverse. Ordinary interactions within the church, workplace, and neighborhood hence tended to put people in touch with others who were in many other respects unlike themselves.[92] They shared one social identity in common, but nonetheless remained diverse in many other respects.

Today, things have changed. Our various social identities are now tightly contained within partisan identity.[93] Again, partisan affiliates tend not only to share a common political perspective; they also embrace a common lifestyle and inhabit the same social worlds. As a result, casual encounters are increasingly likely to occur only among citizens who are politically alike.

This brings us to the nearby phenomenon of political saturation. With partisan affiliation expanded into a lifestyle, more and more of what we do has become an expression of our politics.[94] Yes, liberals carry tote bags and conservatives wear camo. But, importantly, they do these things partly to *live* their politics, to *enact* their partisan membership. Of course, these behaviors also serve to *communicate* partisan affiliation to others. Living one's politics is also a matter of being *recognized* as an affiliate by one's allies and foes. Thanks to partisan sorting, then, the entire social environment has become like the stadium on gameday, except that it is organized around partisan tribes—thus also partisan enmity—rather than sports teams.

Liberals and conservatives embrace distinct lifestyles. As a result, their different ways of life have become saturated with expressions of partisanship. Ordinary activities are now permeated with political meaning.[95] Everything from shopping for groceries, enjoying a genre of music, eating at a particular fast-food chain, ordering a specific brand of beer, and relaxing on a beach is now so strongly correlated with our politics that they have become ways of *communicating* our politics and *affirming* our partisan selves.[96]

To be clear, there's nothing wrong with wanting to live according to one's convictions. But notice that in order to serve as affirmations of our partisanship, these modes of social behavior must be *legible* to others as markers of our political identity. When seeking this kind of validation, we must behave in ways that are recognized as characteristic for those who embrace our partisan identity. In other words, carrying a tote bag or wearing a camo shirt has the expressive significance it does *because* people generally recognize such acts as partisan signals. In this way, political saturation has a homogenizing effect, too. As our partisan identities become centered, we grow increasingly more like our allies across an expanding range of behaviors. Crucially, though, this homogenization doesn't *feel* like compliance. Political saturation makes partisan conformity feel like authentic self-expression.

Naturally, these signals of partisan identity invite certain encounters and discourage others. And given that social space is already segregated according to partisan affiliation, the result is that our daily routines increasingly place us in interaction only with those who share our political identity. Now remember our account of belief polarization: As our partisan identities have grown so central to our overall sense of ourselves, these casual interactions corroborate our political stance, which initiates belief polarization. Observing a fellow Whole Foods shopper carrying an MSNBC tote affirms one's liberal identity, and hence can prompt belief polarization. The same goes for the conservative who encounters a fellow citizen dressed in camo in a Walmart.

The combination of sorting and saturation makes partisan identity perpetually salient. Our partisan selves are thereby triggered, and thus centered. This means that our everyday interactions prompt us to view our relations to others through the lens of the categories and fissures supplied by our partisanship. Given the Corroboration View of belief polarization, the centering of our partisan selves exposes us to extremification and homogenization specifically with respect to our political identity. In this way, sorting and saturation do not only organize our lives around partisanship; they also *shrink* our social worlds into political enclaves.[97] These consolidations then serve to further center our partisan selves.

We have found the needed link between belief polarization and affective polarization. Our social environments are structured in ways that center our partisan selves, consolidating entire lifestyles around politics. This centering leads to belief polarization within our political coalitions. Belief polarization causes us to become more extreme in our political ideas, but also more conformist with respect to our partisan allies. Thus, our desire to fit in with our allies escalates. As a result of this, our negative stance towards perceived partisan foes intensifies. In the interest of garnering validation from our allies, we routinely engage in behavior that expresses our contempt for partisan outsiders. Our political alliances thereby become more hivelike and disassociated from nonmembers, which in turn fosters further belief polarization and thus affective polarization within them.

We have been exploring the puzzle of why in the United States affective polarization has radically intensified in the absence of a corresponding deepening of partisan divisions over political policy. We now have an answer. The related phenomena of sorting and saturation focus the forces of belief polarization specifically on our political coalitions. Belief polarization prompts escalating negative affect towards an out-group, so when it is prevalent within our political alliances, affective polarization is among its effects. In other words, when the partisan self is centered, belief polarization produces affective polarization. Indeed, given how belief polarization works, when social environments are sorted and saturated, we should *expect* affective polarization to escalate regardless of differences over political policy.

3.4 The Polarization Dynamic

The problem of polarization now can be stated succinctly. With our social spaces sorted and saturated according to partisan identity, belief polarization and political polarization work together in a self-perpetuating dynamic. This dynamic deforms our views about our partisan opponents and their views, needlessly aggravating our differences. Additionally, it rewards divisiveness among public officials, thereby incentivizing political obstruction and inflexibility. But perhaps most importantly, the polarization dynamic erodes the ethos of civility by dismantling our ability to understand and reflect upon others' perspectives; it thus undermines our capacity to treat our fellow citizens as our equals.

3.4.1 How the Dynamic Works

To see how the dynamic works, start with our belief polarized political coalitions. We have seen that as we extremify within our partisan enclaves, we also escalate our animosity toward political outsiders. As we shift, their perspectives look increasingly disfigured, unfounded, and irrational. Those who embrace such views begin to strike us as ignorant, naïve, and threatening. We come to see them collectively as a radicalized monolith unified around the most extreme versions of the views that oppose our own. Additionally, because partisanship has expanded into a lifestyle, more of what they do strikes us as explicable by reference to their depraved political perspective. We see them as not only misguided politically, but also wholly corrupt people. We begin to treat a person's opposing partisan affiliation as a sufficient reason to write them off entirely.[98]

As a result, we disengage from partisan outsiders and more thoroughly embed with our allies. Our social world shrinks, and thus partisan identity is further centered. This instigates further belief polarization, which both escalates our negative stance toward outsiders and intensifies conformity pressures among our allies. Maintaining clear boundaries between our partisan friends and foes hence becomes paramount. Expressing contempt for the opposing side becomes a dependable way to assure to allies of one's authentic membership in the group, and in return those expressions are validated by the group. Affective polarization thereby intensifies further.

Meanwhile, we become less tolerant of deviations from our group's predominant expectations. Our partisan coalitions hence begin to demand alignment on a range of arguably unrelated political stances.[99] We thus grow more groupish and homogeneous in lifestyle. Members begin to line up on matters that extend far beyond politics. Again, this permeation shrinks our social world to the point where we interact only with others who are just like us.

Now, it might seem that this combination of belief and affective polarization is politically beneficial. One might think that heightened solidarity and commitment within a political coalition is generally a good thing. If they are to be effective, political coalitions need to be mobilized, and that's what belief and affective polarization achieve. But here's the problem. This combination of escalating in-group partisan affinity and contempt for the political opposition is especially hazardous. It is positively correlated with the view that violence is an acceptable means for achieving one's political ends.[100] Note the tragic irony. As we come to regard our opponents in increasingly unflattering ways, we come to fit the description we ascribe to them. *We* grow more insular, monolithic, militant, and divested from democracy.

In addition to being dysfunctional, the interplay of belief and affective polarization is also degenerative. Once belief polarization and affective polarization have escalated, it's difficult to dial them back. After all, these forces make our behavior *reflexive*, aimed at fitting in with our allies. Accordingly, they render us less able to competently reflect on our partisanship. Hence, at a certain level of belief and affective polarization, amiable interactions with moderate political opponents tend to feed our extremity.[101] Attempts to find common ground backfire.[102] We become more susceptible to group-affirming misinformation, and more adept at rationalizing in the face of new information.[103] Even our perceptions of ordinary political conditions—from the state of the economy and the extent of immigration to the effectiveness of COVID vaccination—are processed in ways that confirm our biases against partisan foes.[104]

Our partisan rivals are subject to the same forces. They also extremify, homogenize, insulate, and demonize. They begin to view the world through the lens of their own partisanship. A sadly self-fulfilling projection results: each side shifts towards its opposition's most unflattering caricature. Oddly, the perception gap closes, because each side comes to fit the deformities the other side had ascribed to them. And, ironically, as their divisions intensify, the opposing sides become more alike—they both grow similarly antidemocratic.

So far, we have focused mainly on how the polarization dynamic warps relations among political rivals. But remember that belief polarization also disfigures our relations with our allies. It homogenizes our coalitions. To repeat, as coalitions belief polarize, they not only become more internally alike, but they also become more committed to their alikeness, more *conformist*. Belief polarization hence leads us to demand of our allies an exaggerated degree of unanimity across a widening range of matters. It therefore causes us to shrink our conception of the range of acceptable difference among our associates. As we grow more inclined to disengage from our foes, we also become less able to acknowledge our friends as our equals. Just as we come to see our rivals as mere obstacles, we also come to see our allies merely as tools that serve our ends. For this reason, heavily belief polarized alliances tend to factionalize and eventually fracture.[105]

So much for the effects of belief polarization and affective polarization within and across our partisan alliances. Consider next how the dynamic works with respect to the remaining facets of political polarization. We noted earlier that the affective, elite, and platform sites of political polarization are mutually reinforcing. So when the citizenry is segregated into partisan tribes that despise each other, candidates and officials are incentivized to amplify their disdain for their opponents.[106] Recall that citizens with high levels of cross-partisan contempt are more likely to vote.[107] Moreover, negative affect for the opposing party is a reliable trigger of various other forms of political behavior.[108] Thus, affective polarization incentivizes, reinforces, and rewards elite polarization. For the same reason, parties do well to fixate on intransigence and obstruction. Intensifications of platform polarization result.

That's the polarization dynamic. In a nutshell: under conditions of sorting and saturation, belief polarization drives affective polarization, which in turn incentivizes both elite and platform polarization. What's more, these tendencies are mutually reinforcing. As citizens grow more extreme and hivelike in their partisan identities, their negative affect for opposing partisans escalates. This in turn provides politicians and parties an easy strategy for gaining and maintaining political power—they simply need to stoke cross-partisan animosity. This encourages citizens to further embed within their partisan enclaves, which further centers their partisan selves. This then provokes further belief and affective polarization.[109] And on it goes.

3.4.2 The Real Problem of Polarization

The general character of the polarization dynamic is clear enough. Let's now specify the problem it poses for democracy.

The polarization dynamic suggests that our partisan stances are products of social and cognitive forces that warp our grasp of our political circumstances. These forces lead us to systematically *misconstrue* our fellow citizens' perspectives, values, and priorities. We come to see them and their commitments as more radical, militant, ungrounded, and distant than they in fact are. This threatens democracy because responsible citizenship requires us to be responsive to the positions that our fellow citizens *actually hold*. Accordingly, existing degrees of political animosity are pathological not because animosity is unpleasant, but rather because it is mistargeted, rooted in deformed caricatures of our fellow citizens that we cannot easily dispel.

The polarization dynamic thus undermines civility. It renders us less capable of public-minded, responsive, and transparent political advocacy. As it leads us to regard our partisan foes as antidemocratic threats to be neutralized, the polarization dynamic encourages the view that perspectives that differ from our own are depraved, groundless, and incoherent. It thereby dismantles our ability to see things from any standpoint other than our own. Moreover, it transforms our partisan coalitions into groups that *valorize* myopic alignment with one's allies. Yet, as we have seen, civility involves various forms of imaginative perspective-taking and efforts at sympathetic understanding of others' perspectives.

Therefore, polarization thwarts the democratic aspiration by eroding the capacities within us that are required for proper citizenship.

In response to this corrosion of civility, candidates, officeholders, and parties respond accordingly. Indeed, because polarization simplifies electoral and campaign strategizing, political parties and candidates *benefit* from the polarization dynamic; so they feed it. They exaggerate their cross-partisan enmity, valorize in-party purity, and stigmatize cooperation with the other side. Democracy hence becomes absorbed by the familiar patterns of tribal combat, where the central political goal among the parties is overcoming the other side. As a result, exercises of political power become merely coercive, impositions of brute force among equals. The democratic aspiration thus recedes. *That's* the problem of polarization.

It should be emphasized that this account of the polarization problem departs significantly from the popular understanding of polarization that was discussed at the start of this chapter. To put the difference most starkly, the popular account locates polarization within the hostile relations between partisan adversaries; it therefore sees polarization as a problem *across* our political divides. By contrast, the account we have developed says that the problem of polarization lies *within* us and *among* our allies.

To add some detail, note that our view does not suggest that the problem of polarization lies with the depth or rancor of our partisan divisions. It invokes no "both sides" premise and does not assume that belief polarization is symmetrical across partisan divisions. Nor does it suggest that once the polarization dynamic has been tamed, citizens will find that their political differences are trivial. It does not urge citizens to reconcile or find common ground. It does not valorize harmony and consensus. To repeat, the problem of polarization is that problem of *misdirected* political animosity, *misconstrued* partisan divides, and *manufactured* policy rifts.

Still, one might conclude that the polarization problem as we have presented it is abstract, and perhaps for that reason of little import. We have said that polarization is a problem because it detracts from the grand aspiration for a society of self-governing equals. Yet that aspiration is undeniably remote, even under less polarized conditions. What's more, our society is overrun with obstacles to democracy—political corruption, gerrymandering, corporate influence, social inequality, voter suppression, and so on. Given the full inventory of challenges that our democracy currently faces, perhaps polarization is not much of a problem at all.

So let's take a moment to bring the problem of polarization down to Earth. We have said that polarization is a problem because it erodes our capacities for civility. This erosion creates significant material difficulties in the here-and-now of democratic politics. To see this, consider that our democracy presently confronts momentous political challenges. These range from global issues of climate change, large-scale migration, public health, and terrorism to relatively local matters including misinformation, mass incarceration, poverty, and racism. In addition, there are new questions on the horizon involving Artificial Intelligence and other recent technologies—difficulties whose shape is not yet apparent.

Dealing with any of these challenges will take concerted effort on the part of citizens and their governments. And given that many of these matters are largely unprecedented, addressing them competently will likely require that we develop novel conceptual tools and new political vocabularies. We will have to *think differently* in order to tackle these problems. But insofar as it centers our partisan selves, the polarization dynamic reinforces established political categories, familiar scripts, and common group dispositions. It prompts our established partisan reflexes and favors instantaneous political verdicts, all at the expense of reflection and imagination.

In this sense, polarization stands in the way of progress. It tethers us to a political vernacular that reinforces longstanding partisan habits. It therefore dooms us to a politics that is organized around the fissures and rivalries that are artifacts of our past, a politics driven by longstanding patterns of partisan resentment and indignation. When our democracy is fixated on entrenched grievance, we lose the capacity to envision a political future that looks different from our present, a future where our political circumstances will have changed not because we will have finally vanquished our partisan foes, but rather because partisan identities and the political formations that surround them have been transformed. In short, the polarization dynamic thus locks us into our existing political idiom.

Arguably, this longstanding vernacular and the habits that it encourages are partly the reason why so many of the most urgent political issues of our day seem hopeless and intractable. But now is not the time for politics as usual. To repeat, we presently confront challenges that call for new ways of thinking, for political imagination and conceptual innovation. Insofar as our democracy is in the grip of the polarization dynamic, our politics will be captured by existing partisan configurations. Our democracy thus is fated to buttress the scaffolding that keeps the dynamic running. Accordingly, unless the polarization dynamic is disrupted, democracy will be conducted by means of the very categories that need to be surpassed.

An additional point is in order. Recall that elected officials, parties, and candidates all benefit from the polarization dynamic. It releases officeholders from the ordinary electoral pressures to produce actual results and allows them to campaign simply on the basis of partisan indignation. What's more, given that the citizenry is already disposed to lay the blame for our political dysfunctions strictly on their partisan opponents, lamenting our polarized condition is itself an effective way for politicians to mobilize their base. Complaining about polarization fuels polarization. In short, the polarization dynamic makes politics easier for politicians and their parties—it works in their favor.

This is why we must look elsewhere for the required interventions. To be clear, addressing the polarization problem will likely require broad changes in our political institutions and practices. At the very least, we will have to constrain the influence of money in our politics; we must loosen the ties between democracy and commerce. But more sweeping changes to our electoral processes and government structures may also be needed. Yet we need not delve into these matters here. Our present point is this: given that politically powerful agents benefit from the status quo, we should not expect them to introduce the needed large-scale modifications.

To return to a point made in Chapter 1, not every big problem can be addressed with a similarly sized remedy. In order make institutional changes, we first need to pave the way. This involves altering the conditions that make our polarized condition beneficial to those who hold power. And that alteration lies with us, the citizens. More precisely, it lies *within* us, with our own civic dispositions and habits. Accordingly, the prescription we will develop in the next chapter is decidedly *local*, aimed at identifying small, accessible steps citizens can take to address polarization and recover civility.

3.5 Democracy's Autoimmune Disorder

But before turning to a discussion of our prescription, we need to recall that addressing the polarization dynamic is not a straightforward task. We cannot prescribe that citizens stop engaging in the kind of behavior that exposes them to the polarization dynamic. This is because the polarization dynamic arises *internally*. It does not emerge from our democratic failings; it is not the product of antidemocratic forces. Rather, the dynamic has its origins in our earnest attempts to meet our civic responsibilities. We find ourselves caught in the polarization dynamic partly because citizenship is a morally conflicted office. Responsible citizenship requires forms of political activity that can dismantle our capacities for civility. As we put it earlier, democracy is subject to an autoimmune disorder.

It is worth spelling this thought out in greater detail. Recall the conception of responsible citizenship proposed in Chapter 2. There, we found that citizens must take responsibility for their democracy. They must be *participants* in the activities of self-government. But to have an effective voice in a modern democratic society, one must join a choir. Responsible citizenship involves sharing ideas with likeminded others, building coalitions, mobilizing one's allies, and engaging in collective political activities.

So far, so good. Yet, in addition to taking responsibility for their democracy, citizens also have a responsibility to one another. Democratic citizenship is also a matter of recognizing the political equality of one's fellow citizens. Our political activity thus must be responsive to the values, objectives, and priorities of our democratic partners. Among other things, we must try to see things from perspectives that differ from our own. In other words, recognizing the political equality of our fellow citizens requires more than a "live and let live" posture of noninterference; we must endeavor to render their standpoint *comprehensible* to us, even though we might nonetheless regard it as misguided or even wrong. This calls for exercises of the imagination, attempts to place ourselves in others' shoes, so to speak. Responsible citizenship thus goes beyond collective political action. It also involves distinctive modes of political reflection.

And there's the rub. Democratically essential forms of collective political participation expose us to forces that systematically distort our perceptions of our fellow citizens. What's more, those distortions tend to be difficult to dislodge. Once in place, they are self-reinforcing. They erode our capacity to treat our perceived political opponents as our equals. In this way, characteristically democratic action undermines our capacity for democratic reflection. Yet those modes of action nonetheless are required for responsible citizenship. In taking responsibility for our democracy, we damage our capacity to meet our responsibilities to our fellow citizens. Acts of responsible citizenship can be hazardous to democracy's health.

This is why our response to the polarization dynamic can't be to simply do *more* of the things that we typically associate with proper citizenship, even if we also do them *better*. In fact, we have seen that under existing circumstances, simply doing more of what we are already inclined to do is likely to be counterproductive—our political circumstances are configured in ways that reinforce the polarization dynamic. To repeat, the polarization problem is not a matter of a democratic *deficit* that can be resolved with redoubled effort. We cannot eliminate the cause of polarization. We thus cannot cure our democracy of it. Instead, we must manage polarization. The question is how.

4
The Need for Solitude

Here's where things stand. The social environment is politically sorted and saturated. Our partisan selves have been centered. Our thinking has been captured by the resulting cognitive and affective distortions. Ordinary avenues of democratic remediation are structured by categories and institutional forms that perpetuate the very pathologies we must try to disrupt. Under these conditions, otherwise commendable civic practices mobilize our worst political tendencies, thus undercutting the democratic aspiration. Moreover, politically powerful agents reap substantial benefits from the status quo.

This picture is undeniably sobering. What's worse, a disconcerting possibility lurks. It could be that democracy's autoimmune disorder has advanced to the point of terminality. Perhaps our democracy is fated to undermine itself from within.

That's a bleak conclusion. We need not resign ourselves to it just yet. Still, we mustn't simply dismiss this possibility, either. The idea that it might be too late to constrain the polarization dynamic is crucial for our thinking about how to proceed. This is because it contains the suggestion that managing polarization calls for us to do something different. Given that the polarization problem is a byproduct of otherwise essential democratic activity, our response cannot be to do *more* of what we are already doing. We need to do democracy *better*. And the bleak conclusion clears the ground for the further thought that in order to do democracy better, we must do something *new*.

To sharpen this connection, recall the remedial nature of our enterprise. The aim is to prescribe restorative action in light of democracy's troubled condition. To this end, we surveyed a range of empirical findings and formulated a diagnosis: our democracy is faltering because the polarization dynamic has intensified to a pathological degree. The prescription now seems obvious. We need to manage polarization.

That's true. But what can we do? Before answering, remember the Curative Fallacy. In developing a prescription, we must keep in mind that remediation is different from prevention. Our aim is not simply to discern how citizens might have suppressed the polarization dynamic. We are not seeking to identify how citizens should have been interacting all along, so that we might induce them to interact in that way now.

This is because the question of what to do in response to our problem is not adequately answered by an account of how we might have averted it. Although it might be a good idea to begin acting in ways that would have kept the polarization dynamic within workable limits, we are attempting to mitigate polarization that already exists, not prevent it. Given that this particular dysfunction is *internal* to the office of citizenship, we cannot simply eradicate its causes. Instead, our strategy is to explore remedial possibilities that lie outside of our usual practices.

Proceeding in this way does not mean that we should abandon our familiar democratic activities. Our objective is not to *replace* the typical requirements of citizenship, but to *supplement* them. This points toward an expanded conception of civic responsibility. Citizens must practice civility. But that's not all. In order to do democracy better, they must do something more, something in addition to the customary.

Our thesis is that this additional and unfamiliar form of democratic activity calls for solitude. Here's the thumbnail of the argument. Because our social surroundings are already primed to fuel the polarization dynamic, citizens need to rehabilitate their capacities for democratic reflection in settings that are detached from that ecosystem. They must enact modes of political reflection that are disconnected from the partisan provocations that structure their ordinary social settings. This calls for *social* distance from our political friends and foes. But that's not all. We will see that managing polarization also involves a kind of *conceptual* distance, the contemplation of political circumstances that are alien to our own. This conceptual distance is possible only when we engage with political perspectives that are not readily translatable into our partisan idiom. Briefly put, to do democracy better, we must decenter our partisanship, and this can be done by exercising cognitive and affective capacities in settings that force us to see past ourselves.

The underlying thought is that in order to restore our democratic capacities, we need to remind ourselves that it's not all about us, right here and now. This may sound strange. Democracy is rule by the people. It is popular self-government among equals, in the here-and-now. Given that our society confronts a range of urgent political challenges that demand cogent responses, there is an obvious sense in which democracy *is* all about us.

Fair enough. But consider that democracy is more than the mechanisms of collective decision-making. It is fundamentally an *aspiration*. Democracy thus extends beyond our current circumstances. To paraphrase John Dewey at his best, democracy is a creative endeavor that's always stretched out before us.[1] That's simply what an aspiration *is*—a forward-looking enterprise. Thus, even though our political action must be directed to the present, our political thinking must aim at a collective future that now can only be imagined. We must confront current challenges while also projecting a future social landscape that is fundamentally different from our own. To accomplish this, we must stretch our democratic vistas beyond the boundaries of our contemporary political vernacular. Our thesis is that this enlargement of our democratic thinking requires civic solitude.

This chapter explores this proposal. I again emphasize that this prescription is speculative. More precisely, it is a conjecture developed out of our analysis of the nature and mechanisms of the polarization dynamic. As such, it is offered as something for citizens to *try* in light of the alarming condition of our democracy.

As noted previously, the prescription runs contrary to common views of civic responsibility. The idea that the civic is inherently public and collective runs deep in our political consciousness, as does the corollary view that nonpublic and solitary activities are therefore also non-civic. So building the case for civic solitude requires that we proceed judiciously. To begin, we will need to examine a more familiar strategy for managing polarization. We will eventually also have to discuss the ways in which familiar kinds of shared space—parks, museums, libraries—have come to be understood as community amenities rather than settings for essential democratic activity. But before starting down this path, let's develop the argument for expanding our conception of our civic responsibilities. To do this, we need to revisit the account developed in Chapter 2.

4.1 Expanding Civic Responsibility

Return to the Google search for the phrase "this is what democracy looks like." Select your favorite image. If it's possible, choose one in which the group is advocating for a policy that you in fact support. Now place yourself in the picture—imagine yourself taking part in the demonstration.

So there you are. You're in a public space, acting in concert with a large number of likeminded citizens for a common cause. Like many of the others, you're holding a sign that both communicates your stance and assures others of your allyship. You are wearing apparel or colors that are linked to your coalition. In addition, you are marching in step with your partners. Perhaps there is a high-profile member of the group with a bullhorn who is leading the collective in a chant, song, or characteristic gesture. There's a lot of choreographed behavior going on. Yet it doesn't feel like conformity. You haven't joined a herd. Rather, you and your allies are presenting a unified front on behalf of justice as you understand it.

If you have ever participated in a large-scale political demonstration, you probably know how exhilarating it can be. There's a distinctive rush one gets when standing up with allies for what one thinks is right. The thrill is amplified when the collective action is staged in a highly visible setting with large numbers of people. It feels good to be seen when making a stand. The combination of affirmation and solidarity is elevating. It's easy to get wrapped up in the elation.

Perhaps this is why people sometimes describe themselves as "hooked" on political activism. But let's suppose that you're not motivated solely by the emotional jolt that comes with mass social action. Instead, your fundamental motives are civic. You showed up for the demonstration seeking to hold government to account. You aim to promote justice, to make a positive difference to your society. You're demonstrating in order to take responsibility for democracy.

Good for you. Yet democracy is not only a matter of showing up. It demands more. In addition to being active, we must also be thoughtful and reflective. This is because when we engage in political advocacy, whether in the voting booth or on the public square, we are exercising political power. Even though we each wield only a sliver of power, it nonetheless must be exercised with care. Responsible citizenship thus requires a modest degree of political competence. Our political actions must be reasonably informed, or at least not oblivious. For this reason, democracy asks that we take steps to understand the political issues that our society must address.

Suppose that you did your homework. Before deciding to join the demonstration, you gathered information, examined the issue, weighed the different feasible policy options, and reached your position in a reasonable way. We can go further to say that in thinking through the matter at hand, you sought not merely to identify the policy that would best advance your personal interests; rather, you considered the matter from the perspective of the *public* good. In this way, your advocacy reflects your sincere judgment about what's best for everyone.

Again, that's all to the good. But democratic citizenship makes further demands. In addition being competent and concerned with the public good, we also have the distinctive responsibility to treat our fellow citizens as our equals. This means that while deciding what political decisions are best, we must ask ourselves what we can rightfully impose on them, given their values, concerns, and priorities. As our fellow citizens are our equals, they get to exercise their own judgment and reach their own political conclusions. Accordingly, we must be able to formulate a rationale for our political advocacy that reflects a sincere engagement with their perspectives. As it was put in Chapter 2, we must promote conditions under which citizens can be political critics rather than mere complainers.

Thus, a central part of recognizing their equality lies in making the effort to understand where our fellow citizens are coming from. To exhibit due regard for our democratic partners, we must try to see things from where they stand. This is especially important when their ideas run contrary to our own.

You are at the demonstration. You've done your homework. Your advocacy reflects a responsible judgment about what policy best serves the public good. Now let's suppose that you've also considered the commitments that animate those on the other side of the issue. Your stance is informed not only by your earnest thinking about the public good, but also by a sincere attempt to grapple with the perspectives of your fellow citizens, including those who are your rivals. You thus have grasped their positions, and you also can explain your stance in terms that your opponents could comprehend and contest. You are exercising your political power in a way that is non-subordinating.

You thereby have satisfied the demands of civility. And that's definitely to your credit. Now here's the catch. Our analysis of polarization suggest that something remains undone. Given the circumstances we have documented, there is reason to suppose that your political stance may be driven by the polarization dynamic. Indeed, we saw that certain distortions in political thinking are positively correlated with being a well-informed and active citizen.[2] This is not to say that your opinions are wrong or unfounded. Nor is it to say that your judgment definitely has been impaired by polarization. But it is to say that there is a compelling reason to view yourself as *vulnerable* to polarization's distortions.

A new difficulty comes to light. Although we readily can identify polarization in our foes, the impacts of the dynamic are hard to detect in our own case. We rarely see our own dispositions as ill-founded or misdirected. And almost no one walks around believing that their own political commitments are the products of distorting dynamics. Instead, we tend to see ourselves as well informed, appropriately responsive to the facts, and fair minded. Again, although the forces of polarization lead us to extremify and homogenize in ways that do not reflect our evidence, we ordinarily don't perceive the group dynamics in ourselves. From the inside, the shifts associated with polarization feel like authentic self-expression.

So we tend to see the polarization problem in strictly second- and third-personal terms. We point to our partisan adversaries—either individually or collectively—and declare that *they're* in the grip of polarization's distortions. Notice how much of popular partisan commentary proceeds mainly by way of imputing delusions, derangements, and naïvetés to the other side. In extreme cases, commentators describe their partisan opposition as a "gullible" and "brainwashed" mob, or a "cult" awash in "fake news" and an "alternate reality." More importantly, the opposition's susceptibility to polarization is our preferred explanation of why they're so politically clueless. We regard polarization as *their* problem. More precisely, we see polarization as the problem *with* them.

Things are different in our own case. When considering our own political commitments, our thinking goes in the other direction. Whereas we see our opposition's misguided political ideas as the products of their cognitive and affective weakness, we regard the soundness of our political commitments as a kind of inoculation against polarization. In other words, we think that because our political views are well founded, we are invulnerable to polarization's distortions.

But this is a mistake. To be sure, it's important to believe what's true (or at least to avoid believing what's false). But what counts for responsible citizenship is the capacity to form political judgments on the basis of good reasons. We have seen that belief polarization is not reason-responsive; it is driven by social dynamics among peers. Moreover, no evidence suggests that having correct political commitments renders one any less vulnerable to the polarization dynamic. Again, part of the problem of polarization is that it is largely invisible from the first-personal perspective. Belief and affective polarization are stealthy. This is what makes managing them so challenging.

Consider the result. The ordinary activities of responsible democratic citizenship expose us to cognitive and affective forces that warp our political judgment and erode our capacities for civility. But those forces are difficult to detect in our own case. In fact, it may be that they thrive specifically because they're stealthy. But leave that thought aside for now. The crucial point is this: it's generally the case that when we have a responsibility to perform a given task, we thereby also have additional responsibilities to preserve the conditions under which we can perform that task reasonably well.

For illustration, think of airline pilots. Their job is to safely transport passengers. Accordingly, their work is governed by a catalogue of safety precautions. In addition to routine protocols for checking the plane's operational systems before taking flight and so on, pilots are also subject to constraints on the number of consecutive hours they can fly. They are required to *rest* after a certain period of time.

Notice how this latter requirement points to a more general responsibility. Pilots have an obligation to preserve their capacities for alertness, acuity, and overall dependable flying. We can say that their responsibility to provide safe transport entails duties to maintain the requisite faculties. For one thing, they must routinely monitor their health; they need to regularly have their vision and hearing checked, for example. They are also obligated to take steps to counteract forces that can weaken the needed capacities. Among other things, they must take care to get sufficient sleep. They have a further duty to remove sources of undue distraction from their work environment. Overall, they need to guard against tendencies that would cause them to lose focus during flight.

This means that being a good pilot takes more than compliance with the official regulations and protocols. It also requires a regimen of self-monitoring. Responsible pilots routinely scrutinize their own habits with a view toward adjusting their practices in ways that better enable them to perform well as providers of safe air transport. Of course, pilots are not required to *maximize* their effectiveness in the cockpit. They needn't orient their entire lives for *optimal* piloting. But they do need to preserve certain threshold capacities necessary for *good*—or, at the very least, *adequate*—performance. In this way, responsible piloting is partly a matter of *internal* regulation.

Responsible citizenship is not much different. It's our civic job to contribute to collective self-government among equals. Performing well in this role calls for civility. However, we have seen that our sorted and saturated environments tend to undercut the democratic character of our political activities, transforming otherwise responsible democratic behavior into fuel for the polarization dynamic. We thus have an obligation to preserve our capacities for civility, the internal conditions that must obtain in order for us to conduct ourselves reasonably well as citizens. Therefore, we need to take steps to keep polarization in check.

With this thought in hand, let's return to the political demonstration. You are to be commended for satisfying the requirements of civility. Still, you are also aware that you are subject to cognitive and affective tendencies that negatively impact the democratic character of your political judgment. These tendencies drive you to be overconfident in your opinions, while also leading you to misconstrue the views of others. But that's not all. They intensify your negative dispositions toward those who do not share your political commitments; they also escalate your inclination to conform to your allies' expectations. And these forces are difficult to detect in yourself. All told, you are subject to subtle dynamics that center your partisan self and thereby distort your grasp of your political circumstances.

If you showed up at the demonstration without having taken steps to mitigate these effects, your advocacy is less commendable than it could have been. The democratic quality of your engagement is in question. This is true even if it turns out that your perspective hasn't been significantly warped by affective and belief polarization. Again, the fact that you are aware of your *vulnerability* to distorting forces is enough to trigger the responsibility to take precautions to keep them in check. Just as the pilot must rest after an assigned number of hours regardless of how she might assess her alertness, citizens must introduce measures designed to counteract polarization. This is all the more evident in light of the fact that polarization is stealthy. We need to subject our democratic capacities to routine maintenance, even when we have no special reason to think they've been compromised. That's a requirement of responsible citizenship, too.

The ethos of civility therefore does not exhaust our civic responsibilities. Because we must advocate civilly, we are also obliged manage polarization. So we have a responsibility to introduce civic practices that can address polarization. Like the pilots, we need to check ourselves.

4.2 Managing Polarization

This immediately raises the question of what we must do. Here is one plausible response. The dysfunctions of polarization are most evident in our partisan antagonism; thus the first order of business is to deescalate cross-partisan animosity. After all, when citizens are disposed to see their partisan rivals as depraved enemies of democracy itself, little progress can be made on any other front. To begin to address the polarization problem, then, there must be a change in how citizens regard one another. Specifically, citizens need to learn to see their partisan opponents as democratic partners rather than as civic enemies.

Call this the *relational approach* to managing polarization. Ultimately, we will set this strategy aside, opting instead for an alternative called the *personal approach*. Yet the relational approach is undeniably sensible. We will see that, whatever its merits, it is insufficient as a management strategy. We can better grasp its limitations by looking at a well-developed program that embraces it.

4.2.1 The Relational Approach: Facilitated Democracy

One influential version of the relational approach recognizes that our everyday settings for political interaction are already inundated with triggers for partisan antagonism. It holds that the project of managing polarization thus cannot be left to citizens on their own. Instead, deescalation must be *facilitated*. So researchers and practitioners have devised a variety of inventive mediations, all involving what can be called *curated cross-partisan encounters*. These are specially designed forums where trained personnel guide divided citizens through structured interactions that prompt civil behavior.³

To be sure, the differences among these proposals are significant. Some focus on rehabilitating face-to-face dialogue among partisan adversaries. Others seek explicitly to foster common ground among small partisan groups. Some propose institutional innovations involving the use of deliberative mini-publics and legislative bodies chosen by lottery.⁴ Despite these variations, though, the proposals share the aim of getting partisan rivals to interact in settings where facilitators encourage the kind of cross-partisan attitudes that are appropriate for democratic citizens. Thus we can refer to them collectively as *facilitated democracy* proposals.

The perspective underlying many of these programs is compelling. Drawing from an outlook that goes back at least to Aristotle, facilitated democracy is rooted in the idea that although civility is constituted by habits of thought and feeling that are internal to individual citizens, it is best cultivated by means of interpersonal behavior. Accordingly, facilitated democracy affirms that the way to diminish animosity among citizens is to design forums that incentivize them to interact in ways that are respectful and orderly. The hope is that once civility is implemented under facilitated encounters with their partisan opponents, citizens can bring those practices to their ordinary political interactions.

4.2.1.1 Aristotelian Underpinnings
Let's take a moment to unpack that thought. In his *Nicomachean Ethics*, Aristotle developed a far-reaching theory of what it takes to be a morally good person. His view is thus focused on good *character traits*, stable dispositions to think and feel in ways that are morally admirable. He called these traits *virtues*, and their opposites *vices*. Aristotle hence inaugurated a tradition of moral philosophy that is focused on the moral quality of *persons* rather than of *actions*. According to Aristotle's way of thinking, moral philosophy begins by explaining what makes someone a virtuous

person, and then derives its conception of moral action. On his view, then, an action is moral insofar as it is the kind of thing that a virtuous person would do.[5] This way of proceeding stands in stark contrast to many modern theories of ethics. They tend to begin with an analysis of what makes actions moral, and then define the good person as one who routinely does the moral thing.

We need not get bogged down in the comparative merits of Aristotle's approach to ethics. What's crucial for our purposes is his observation that we acquire virtues by performing virtuous actions.[6] For example, he held that if you seek to become a generous person, you should begin by engaging repeatedly in acts of generosity. Of course, at first those generous acts won't express your personality. You are *becoming* generous—you are not yet a generous person. But Aristotle argued that repeated generous actions instill the virtue of generosity. One acquires the virtue of generosity by doing what a generous person routinely does. Naturally, he proposed the same account of vice. We become, say, *cowardly* by routinely running away from danger.

To get a better grip on this perspective, notice that responsible parenting tends to follow a broadly Aristotelian pattern. Parents browbeat their children into saying "thank you" and "I'm sorry." Of course, authentic expressions of gratitude and apology cannot be the product of browbeating. To count as genuine, they must emerge from *within* the child's own realization that they *owe* an apology or that a token of gratitude is *due*. At first, then, the parent browbeats the child, causing the child to *perform* the acts associated with gratitude and apology. The child thus does not really apologize or thank. But the idea is that performing those acts *instills* the corresponding attitudes, the *internal* tendencies that make saying "I'm sorry" and "thanks" instances of genuine apology and thanking. By *emulating* the behavior of those with the appropriate dispositions, one acquires those dispositions.

Aristotle thus saw morality as a matter of training.[7] Accordingly, he also argued that we need moral exemplars and tutors to train us to be moral. As Aristotle's critics are fond of noticing, this reliance on moral trainers renders the view paternalistic and hierarchical. And perhaps the critics are correct. But we need not pursue that here. The important insight is that when moral training is successful, we *internalize* the appropriate disposition—we acquire the virtue. And once we have acquired the virtue, we do not merely *act* virtuously; rather, virtuous behavior expresses our character. It becomes who we are.

Back now to facilitated democracy. These programs hold that we can reduce partisan animosity by creating occasions where divided citizens are prompted to interact respectfully. Accordingly, facilitated democracy programs invoke ground rules to govern the participants' interactions. Typically, participants are required to remain polite, to listen to others, to take turns speaking, to refrain from using provocative language, and to strive to understand others' perspectives. By following those rules, participants manifest proper civic conduct. And, perhaps with a nod to Aristotle, the expectation is that participants will eventually *internalize* the rules, in which case respectful behavior will become part of their civic character. In this way, the facilitated democracy approach holds that deescalating animosity is the product of civic interpersonal training. Facilitated democracy programs supply the trainers and the training ground.

4.2.1.2 Assessing the Program

Many of the experimental results regarding facilitated democracy are encouraging. There is reason to think that Aristotle was broadly correct: we can ease partisan animosity by interacting across our divides under conditions designed to elicit civil behavior. When divided citizens are brought together in venues that incentivize properly democratic engagement, they seem to be able to set aside their misperceptions and engage respectfully with their opponents. Consider that in a recent self-study, one prominent facilitated democracy group, Braver Angels, reports that 70 percent of participants in their workshops emerge with a "positive view of the other political side," while 80 percent claim that they were able to "find common ground" with partisan opponents.[8]

This is all very promising. Yet the broader data are not entirely affirmative.[9] Some results suggest that facilitated democracy can *exacerbate* patterns of polarization and reinforce negative stereotypes of the opposition.[10] Others have found that respectful engagement with political opponents positively correlates with a *disinclination* to vote.[11] In some cases, it seems that even when facilitated democracy interventions succeed at reducing affective polarization, they do not dispel tendencies to embrace antidemocratic means for defeating political opponents.[12]

Additional research suggests that the encouraging results of facilitated democracy experiments are limited in other ways. For example, the positive effects have been found to apply mainly to subjects who are do not already strongly identify with their political party; when it comes to committed partisans, the impact of facilitated democracy interactions has been found to be modest and fleeting.[13] To be frank, this result is predictable. Facilitated democracy mediations always involve subjects who have volunteered to participate, after all. The subjects of facilitated democracy experiments are thus citizens who already acknowledge the value of the endeavor. Meanwhile, those who are deeply embedded in the polarization dynamic have already written off their rivals. They are unlikely to sign up for an experiment in respecting the other side— they think that the opposition is not worth respecting.

The data are mixed.[14] We should not be surprised by this. Politics is difficult, polarization is multifaceted, and citizens are complicated. Moreover, as our brief survey indicates, there are competing views about how to gauge the success of facilitated democracy interventions. Do we compare participants' pre- and post-intervention attitudes? Do we look to their post-intervention political behavior? Do we simply ask participants whether they enjoyed the process? Thankfully, we need not attempt to sort out these matters here. Our purposes draw us to a limitation of facilitated democracy that derives from the relational approach to polarization management.

In keeping with the relational approach, facilitated democracy programs are almost always explicitly aimed at "finding common ground" and "healing divides" among political opponents. These might be worthy goals. But it is crucial to keep in mind that the polarization problem is *not* simply that our cross-partisan relations are aggravated. Instead, it has to do with distorting tendencies within us that drive us to misconstrue our political circumstances. The problem of polarization resides in forces that *exaggerate* our partisan divides and *misdirect* our antagonism. Yet the facilitated democracy approach treats any reduction in animosity as a democratic success. It regards any bridging of our partisan divide as depolarization.

But it's not true that polarization is diminished whenever citizens deescalate animosity, find common ground, or reach across the divide. This is because polarization involves escalations of both cross-partisan hostility and in-group conformity. As a result, consensus and amicability can be products of polarization, too. Add to this that healthy democracy is inherently contestatory. There are circumstances where civility calls for standing firm, declining compromise, escalating confrontation, doubling-down, and intensifying anger.[15] This is all the more obvious considering the resilience of sites of injustice that continue to plague our society.

In short, managing polarization is not simply a matter of turning down the temperature. A political ecosystem designed to quell rancor and incentivize accord embeds its own democratic hazards. So, in order to make progress in managing polarization, citizens must mitigate their susceptibility to cognitive and affective forces that drive both cross-partisan animosity and in-group conformity. They manage polarization when their partisan zeal and antagonism both are more accurately calibrated, anchored in improved understandings of their fellow citizens' perspectives—political friends and foes alike.

Here, facilitated democracy proponents might refer back to their broadly Aristotelian premises. They may say that the point of the interventions is strictly to elicit the behavior appropriate for responsible citizenship. As the defects in our civic behavior are most prevalent in our cross-partisan relationships, the intervention reasonably aims to rehabilitate those interactions. To repeat, the expectation is that this will eventually instill the corresponding internal dispositions across the range of political conduct.

This may seem like a fitting reply at first, but it actually points to a weakness in the Aristotelian underpinnings of facilitated democracy. Aristotle's view of moral development is aimed principally at persons who do not yet have stable character traits. As suggested by our earlier example of parents and children, his theory is directed toward those who are still *developing* their moral character. The account thus does not address people who already have *vicious* dispositions. It is not a theory of how *bad* people can become good. It therefore is also not an account of how we can *remediate* entrenched corrupt civic habits.

But that's where we find ourselves. The task of rehabilitating civility does not start from scratch, but rather from ground zero. It begins within a scene in which our civic capacities have been under attack. So it is not like the project of instilling good dispositions in children whose characters are yet unformed. Rather, managing polarization begins with citizens who have been operating under circumstances that have fostered uncivil dispositions. In this way, managing polarization has more to do with counteracting civic vices than instilling civic virtues. It's not clear what the Aristotelian approach has to offer us.

Notice next that facilitated democracy stages its interventions explicitly around existing partisan categories. Citizens enter into these forums with their partisan identities overtly primed. They participate *as* liberals or conservatives, Democrats or Republicans.

This is necessary because the entire aim of the relational approach is to nudge citizens into more moderate versions of their partisan selves. Yet by foregrounding the goal of easing divisions, the approach keeps those divisions fully present. It places partisan identity, along with the dominant classifications and vernacular or contemporary politics, at the center. The tendency to see ourselves and our fellow citizens fundamentally through the lens of partisan affiliation ultimately goes unchallenged.

However, we have seen that outside of the facilitated democracy forum, our lives are consolidated around political affiliation. Our friends, families, and workplaces are sorted according to politics, and our social landscape is saturated with partisan signals. We enter into facilitated democracy interventions with our partisan identities already in place. To say the least, the real world of democracy is not optimized for civility. Instead, it is primed to fuel the polarization dynamic. Our partisan identities hence embed uncivil attitudes and habits. Data that we surveyed in the previous chapter suggests that part of what it is to be, say, a liberal is to regard conservatives as generally unfit for citizenship and divested from democracy. Our partisan selves are already pathologized. Spending an afternoon or two sequestered in a setting designed for civility is not likely to counteract the enormous polarizing power of our everyday social settings.

Finally, observe that facilitated democracy programs provide occasions where participants can model civility. They design environments where citizens can interact in ways that *would have* averted the pathological escalation of the polarization dynamic. Accordingly, when it is presented as a sufficient response to polarization, facilitated democracy is entangled in the Curative Fallacy. By contrast, our analysis suggests that if we want to restore our democracy, we need not only to do the familiar activities of citizenship better. We also need to do something new. Facilitated democracy proposes ways to do the usual things better. It is to this extent limited as a strategy for managing polarization.

We must take care not to overstate this conclusion. The result is not that we must reject the facilitated democracy program. Despite the limitations we have noted, it remains plausible to think that facilitated democracy interventions are preferable to doing *nothing*. Indeed, we saw that some data suggest that the interventions are generally effective for citizens who are eager to repair their cross-partisan relations. That facilitated democracy encounters might not be especially impactful for citizens who do not already see their value does not undermine the program. Instead, our result is simply that facilitated democracy is not a panacea. It is insufficient as a strategy for managing polarization. Nevertheless, the struggle for responsible citizenship must be engaged on multiple fronts. Facilitated democracy needn't be abandoned, just supplemented.

4.2.2 Decentering the Partisan Self

The purpose of the foregoing discussion was to bring our positive proposal into focus. Its central contention is that the task of managing polarization is not a matter of repairing cross-partisan hostilities. It instead lies with the fact that the social circumstances within which we must act are already laden with polarization's triggers. As we encapsulated the point earlier, within our saturated and sorted environments, the activities of responsible citizenship *center* our partisan selves. Once partisanship is centered, nearly everything we do serves to amplify our political identity. This is what enables the polarization dynamic to spin out of control. Our management efforts must focus there.

The resulting prescription is plain enough. In order to manage polarization, we need to decenter our partisan selves. This does not mean that we must withdraw from partisan politics. Decentering doesn't mean disengagement. One can remain a committed partisan without permitting partisan identity to envelop the entirety of one's life. Accordingly, the suggestion is that we have a responsibility to counteract the tendency for partisan identity to *consolidate* our lives.

Though the shape of this proposal is straightforward, the idea that we must decenter our partisan selves remains obscure. Clarifying it requires that we take a step back. The idea that the polarization problem lies with the character of our partisan divides needs to be dislodged, and that takes additional effort. Before explaining what decentering amounts to, then, we need to reorient the management task away from the relational and toward the personal.

4.2.2.1 The Personal Approach

To begin, take another look at the relational approach to managing polarization. Specifically, consider its *structure*. It starts by observing that the pathology of polarization is most evident in our toxic political divides. From this, it proposes that managing polarization is a matter of repairing those divides. The inference from the observation to the proposal rests on an intuitive principle: when addressing a dysfunction, one should attend first to its most prominent and debilitating symptoms.

This seems utterly sensible. Yet there's trouble afoot. Despite its appeal, the intuitive principle is not as compelling as one might think. It's not always the case that remedial measures should be targeted at a dysfunction's most evident symptoms. Hence the fact that the problem of polarization manifests in dysfunctional interpersonal relations doesn't mean that our interventions must be focused on repairing them.

To be clear, a healthy democracy is indeed characterized by civil relations across partisan divides, and polarization tends to undermine relations of that kind. Yet it simply doesn't follow that our remediation efforts must aim at deescalating partisan animosity. There is such a thing as treating the symptoms rather than the disease. And there are therapeutic cases where treating the symptoms can exacerbate the underlying pathology. In any case, the relational approach overlooks the possibility that deescalation might be best pursued as a *byproduct* of another kind of mitigation. To manage polarization, we may need to intervene elsewhere.

But where? Recall once again that the polarization problem lies with what *drives* our toxic divisions. As was argued earlier, prevailing degrees of partisan animosity are dysfunctional because they are rooted in polarization's cognitive and affective misrepresentations. Importantly, these warp our capacities to maintain civil relations with our foes and allies alike. In the case of our foes, we attribute exaggeratedly noxious doctrines and attitudes; as for our allies, we insist upon an excessive degree of unanimity. Even though our political divisions are indeed pathological, the management task ultimately must be directed toward our underlying inclinations. As these tendencies are *internal* to us, managing polarization is a matter of self-regulation.

Thus the *personal approach* to polarization management. It sets aside our toxic political relations and locates the task of polarization management within us as individuals. By proceeding in this way, the personal approach need not deny that the health of our democracy depends on deescalating partisan animosity. It holds only that rehabilitating political relations requires us to restore our own civic capacities. Taking a cue from familiar therapeutic strategies that are prominent when dealing with strained relationships of other kinds, it says that to repair our political connections with others, we first need to work on ourselves. We must start small. Civic repair begins with us.

To spell this out, recall polarization's impact on individuals. There isn't need for an extended review of Chapter 3. It is enough to say that these dynamics press us toward greater extremity and conformity while also escalating negative dispositions towards anyone perceived to be different from ourselves. The thing to emphasize at present is that polarization thereby impairs our political judgment. Specifically, the combination of belief and affective polarization artificially inflates our confidence in our perspective. This occurs by means of social pressures to systematically overestimate the force of supporting information and discount invalidating considerations. As it drives us to suppress disagreement and avoid criticism, this overconfidence renders us increasingly dogmatic and impervious to correction.

We noted previously that these tendencies *shrink* our perspective.[16] As our confidence escalates, we become more disposed to regard views that differ from our own as not only mistaken, but unfounded and completely without support. We come to regard others' perspectives as unintelligible. Accordingly, those who do not share our opinions increasingly strike us as deranged and incompetent, not merely wrong. In the end, we come to view those who do not share our partisan identity as incapable of responsible democratic citizenship. We lose sight of the possibility of reasonable political disagreement among sincere citizens.

This condition obviously makes for unhealthy political relations. But we are pursuing the personal approach, so our focus lies elsewhere. Apart from aggravating our interactions with others, polarization makes us worse citizens in a different—and now arguably more important—respect. By dismantling our ability to accurately assess our evidence and understand perspectives that deviate from our own, polarization renders us worse spokespersons for our political views. Consider that as our confidence extends far beyond what our evidence warrants, we become unable to respond adequately to criticism, less adept at revising in light of new information, and more prone to overstating our position. We also begin to embrace caricatures of opposing ideas; thus, we grow incapable of competently critiquing them.

Oddly, as we become more assured of our perspective, we grow less attuned to the reasons that support it. And yet we also become more disposed to insert our politics into everything we do, and to insist that others fall in line. In short, polarization transforms us from advocates into mere advertisers. It thereby diminishes our ability to effectively promote justice. By activating our impulses for political action while simultaneously dismantling our capacities for political reflection, polarization makes us worse at democracy.

Think back to our account of responsible citizenship. Earlier, this account was framed in terms of what we owe to our fellow citizens. But we now see that it goes beyond that. When we practice civility, we do more than recognize the equality of our fellow citizens. We also do our part in promoting a self-governing society of equals. That is, by engaging in responsible citizenship, we further the democratic project. In this way, the ethos of civility orients our political advocacy toward the democratic aspiration.

Insofar as we are invested in that aspiration, the result that polarization impairs our political judgment must strike us as worrisome. It demonstrates that polarization is civically degenerative independently of the toxic character of our cross-partisan interactions. Even if we are inclined to think that our partisan opponents truly are unworthy of civility, polarization remains a problem. This is because it corrupts our capacities for responsible political reflection. It thereby makes us worse at democracy *on the inside*.

Let's draw these threads together. We are aware of our vulnerability to forces that distort our political judgment. We also know that these forces are difficult to detect in our own case. Further, we have seen that this distortion occurs mainly by artificially escalating our confidence in our political perspective. This escalation triggers our disposition to act on behalf of our commitments, while also bypassing our reflective capacities. As our everyday social environments are structured in ways that initiate these forces, we each have reason to suspect that our sense of the warrant for our political judgments is to some extent inflated. We have seen that this inflation not only makes for strained relations among citizens; it also undermines civility by impairing our ability to responsibly advocate for justice. Polarization thus is a personal problem, a problem with each of us.

To solidify this result, think back to the pilots. Given their responsibility to provide safe transport, they have an additional obligation to take reasonable steps to maintain the conditions that enable them to pilot well, or at least adequately. Pilots thus need to monitor themselves and keep track of the state of their capacities. When necessary, they must take precautionary measures to counteract tendencies that would lead to inadequate performance. Responsible piloting is in part a matter of professional *hygiene*.

Similarly, good democratic citizenship involves a regimen of *civic hygiene*. We have a responsibility to monitor and regulate our civic faculties. It falls to us to preserve our democratic aptitudes, and to take steps to counteract factors that degrade them. We are obliged to maintain within ourselves the baseline capacities needed to perform our civic role well, or at least adequately.

So far, so good. Yet the forgoing analysis has shown that our ordinary democratic environments are structured in ways that tend to undercut our civic capacities. We are routinely subject to conditions that instill attitudes and dispositions that fall below a reasonable standard of responsible citizenship. Accordingly, we have the additional obligation to protect, preserve, restore, and fortify the threatened capabilities. This obligation derives simply from our *vulnerability* to the impairments, not from any assessment that our capacities have in fact been significantly corroded. Insofar as we decline to take such steps, we fall short of our civic responsibilities.

In this way, the personal approach locates the problem of polarization centrally in cognitive and affective distortions of our political judgment. It tells citizens that insofar as they care about getting politics right, they have an obligation to protect their faculties from the polarization dynamic. This places the management task on us as individuals.

Before moving on, notice an important contrast between the personal and relational approaches. The relational approach locates the problem of polarization within cross-partisan hostility. It thereby encourages the thought that polarization management involves reconciliation. The personal approach resists this. It holds that, whatever the value of political reconciliation might be, the process of managing polarization is consistent with maintaining a combative stance toward one's partisan opponents. On the account we have developed, partisan relations can remain adversarial, even toxic. Citizens need not seek harmony. We need not endeavor to love our partisan enemies. Managing polarization begins elsewhere.

4.2.2.2 Decentering Explained

Now that the personal approach to polarization management is in place, we can clarify the idea of decentering the partisan self. We have already said that the real culprit in the runaway escalation of the polarization dynamic is the *centering* of partisan identity, the *consolidation* of our lives around political affiliation. When partisan identity is centered, political allyship becomes our principal mode of situating ourselves socially; it dictates our lifestyles and patterns of interaction. The forces that center our partisan selves are thus encoded in our social environments.

That's where the challenge of managing polarization resides. The trouble is that we have little ability to alter the environmental conditions that center our partisan selves. And don't forget that political parties and other powerful agents are the beneficiaries of the status quo. As we noted earlier, the prospects for retrieving democracy seem bleak. Now the prescription emerges: we nonetheless can resist the consolidation of our lives around political identity. We can manage polarization by counteracting the forces that center our partisan selves.

Some readers will hear this proposal as recommending that we "reach across the aisle" and cooperate across our divides. But that's not the idea. It can't be. Those activities keep partisanship securely at the center of everything, whereas our proposal seeks to offset this centrality. Accordingly, decentering focuses on the way the polarization dynamic shrinks our social worlds and our political perspectives. Recall that as our confidence escalates, our sense of the spectrum of reasonable political opinion contracts until it includes only our own. In other words, as partisan identity centers, it increasingly appears to us as the only intelligible stance for a democratic citizen to take. Our prescription, then, is that we dislodge partisan consolidation by expanding our idea of the lifestyle and ideological options that are available to responsible democratic citizens.

It must be emphasized that this is not a call for reconciliation. Coming to see a stance as consistent with responsible citizenship does not amount to accepting it or judging it to be possibly correct. Regarding another's perspective as compatible with the democratic aspiration is not to *credit* it in any way that diminishes our own commitments. In other words, it is possible to regard a political perspective as misguided, ill founded, and flatly incorrect without thereby condemning it as beyond the pale of democracy as such. As we saw in Chapter 2, democracy is premised on the claim that there is a broad spectrum of rival political outlooks that are all consistent with the democratic aspiration. Responsible democratic citizens need not converge on a common political outlook. The democratic aspiration contains multitudes.

When our partisan selves are centered, we lose sight of this foundational democratic premise. We are driven to the view that only those who share our partisan identity are fit for democracy. Decentering, then, is largely a matter of restoring our commitment to the idea that there can be real political opposition *within* the horizon of democracy and *among* responsible citizens. It is the practice of resisting the tendency to cast our political opponents as opponents of democracy as such. In short, decentering involves expanding our democratic palate.

In keeping with the personal approach, decentering begins at home. It proceeds from *within* our partisan standpoint, aiming to dismantle in-group conformity rather than ease out-group antagonism. Accordingly, we decenter our partisan selves by taking steps to validate a broader range of variance *among our allies*, by explicitly acknowledging that allyship does not require across-the-board alignment. Decentering thus involves the de-homogenization of our partisan alliances. It starts with welcoming criticism from our political friends and standing ready to criticism them in return.[17] We thus expand our conception of allyship and begin to restore our commitment to the idea that responsible democratic citizens can differ across a range of ideological and lifestyle matters.

Under healthy democratic conditions, we would be able to decenter by introducing into our coalitions robust Devil's Advocacy norms, practices whereby dissention is explicitly invited from within the group. Alas, present conditions aren't healthy. For those who are especially politically active, partisan networks are already deeply homogenized. Playing Devil's Advocate with your political allies is likely to be counterproductive. It is a good way to raise suspicions about your allyship. Among those for whom partisanship is centered, the very suggestion that there might be something to be said for a diverging viewpoint is likely to be heard as *advocacy* for that viewpoint. And to propose that there might be something of value in the other side's position invites the impression among your allies that you're *on* the other side.

Of course, partisan coalitions vary in these respects. It might be possible to enact practices of internal dissent in some cases. Nevertheless, it's probably wiser to suppose that when it comes to decentering the partisan self, you can't count on your allies to help. You're on your own. Decentering thus does not only begin at home; it also starts within. It calls for an expansion our democratic thinking *from the inside.*

How can we do that? We need to introduce exercises that confront us with the range of responsible political thinking that extends beyond the confines of our partisan identity. Again, were our environments not so thoroughly sorted and saturated, routine activities would expose us to people who impress upon us the breadth of reasonable political difference. But as things stand, day-to-day channels of social interaction tend to reinforce partisan consolidation, they present us with pressures for conformity and prime us to regard divergence from our political views as incompetence and irresponsibility. What is needed, then, is not merely to encounter political difference, but to be exposed to responsible criticism of our own political ideas.

Crucially, the claim here is not that we must adopt the stance that we're fallible, and thus that our beliefs could be wrong. Whatever the merits of that posture might be, the present proposal is that we need occasions for grappling with the various ways in which our ideas can be understood, formulated, assessed, and challenged. In other words, the idea is not that we need greater acquaintance with "pro and con" reasoning that enables us to appreciate "both sides" of the political issues. That keeps partisan identity centered. The idea rather is to expand our conception of democratically permissible political difference within our own perspective.

The proposal is that we can begin to dislodge partisan identity by seeing our ideas as *contestable*, subject to responsible critique. To do that, we needn't come to appreciate merits of our opponents' ideas. We only need to encounter reasons that can be offered against our own. We simply need to see our position as contestable on the basis of *reasons* rather than depravity, misunderstanding, and incompetence.

Taking this perspective on our own ideas is different from adopting the stance that we could be mistaken. Instead, it is to embrace the idea that even if our political ideas are correct and all rivals are wrong, *we* nevertheless could be improved. It is to recognize that our grasp of our own commitments could be enriched, our formulation of our position could be developed, and our arguments could be sharpened. Seeing our views as responsibly contestable is to acknowledge that our political stance admits of variation, and differences in formulation and emphasis. Possibilities for responsible differences *among* our allies thus are opened. We thereby begin to relax the forces of in-group conformity, which in turn expands our political perspective and begins to dislodge partisan consolidation.

Yet we cannot count on others to provide the necessary critical pushback. We are already cued to receive criticism from our opponents as misguided; and our partisan friends are motivated to reinforce group homogeneity. To repeat, when it comes to decentering, we're on our own. So we need to cast ourselves in the contestatory role. We need to turn our faculties of political reflection within and *imagine* how our ideas could be challenged. To decenter the partisan self, then, we need political *self-criticism*.

4.3 Politics Alone

The suggestion that we must engage in political self-criticism instantly raises a new difficulty. We have said that we need to engage in self-criticism because we cannot count on the people around us to supply the pushback necessary for decentering—they're already too submerged in the dynamics of polarization. Yet that same argument seems to apply to ourselves. Our allies and foes are in the grip of polarization, but so are we! When it comes to decentering, we're indeed on our own. But now it looks as if that's a problem. It's likely that our own thinking has been impacted by the forces of extremification and homogenization, and this means that our cognitive and affective faculties are probably keyed to reinforce in-group and out-group boundaries. Why think that we engage in responsible self-criticism?

Maybe we can't. Not as we are, at any rate. We cannot simply step into the role of self-critic. This is because our ordinary environments are inundated with obstacles to honest self-critique, dynamics that merely activate our political reflexes. Given the infiltration of political affiliation into all facets of or social lives, our attempts to be self-critical are likely only to reinforce existing patterns of partisanship. Consequently, adopting the role of political self-critic calls for a special kind of effort.

Thus the central thesis: citizens need to reflect in solitude. Given the forces that shape the world around us, decentering our partisan selves requires that we occasionally *detach* from our ordinary environs, gaining distance from the partisan triggers that saturate our day-to-day lives. Accordingly, the necessary practices of self-critical political reflection call for settings that are removed from our typical sites of social interaction. We need places for civic introspective activity that are nonetheless nonpublic and noncollective. In a slogan, responsible citizenship calls for occasions where we can engage in democratic politics alone. That's civic solitude.

Such is the conjecture that underlies the call for civic solitude. It remains to make the proposal credible. To start, we need to clarify the idea of *distance* that is at work.

4.3.1 Two Kinds of Distance

Although civic solitude calls for a kind of distanced reflection, it is not simply a matter of thinking about politics in isolation. Civic solitude must amount to more than that because our partisan identities can be entrenched under detached conditions, too. Indeed, on many accounts, political radicalization typically occurs when people are secluded. Breaking social ties can be hazardous. Of course, our proposal is not that citizens must wholly disconnect from others, but only that they must *sometimes* think in solitude. Yet one can engage in solitary reflection but still be engrossed in partisan rivalries. Accordingly, civic solitude is a distinctive kind of self-critical activity that is not only isolated, but also *distanced*. The required distance has two aspects: social and conceptual. We'll take these in turn.

Recall the Corroboration View of the mechanism of belief polarization. Extremification and homogenization can be initiated by environmental cues that make our partisan identity salient and then validate our membership with our group. Given this, the need for social distance from other *people*—our political allies and rivals, to be specific—should be clear. Our cognitive and affective tendencies are already primed to reinforce partisan boundaries. Thus the task of dislodging the partisan self needs to be undertaken outside of the interpersonal triggers of in-group conformity and out-group aversion. We cannot engage in political self-criticism under the eye of those who make our partisan identities salient.

This occasions a related point. There's more to social distance than withdrawing from the company of others. We must also gain distance from our ordinary *spaces*. Again, the reason lies with the Corroboration View. It says that although the partisan cues that initiate belief polarization often come from other people, they needn't. The relevant prompts of our partisan reflexes can reside in material features of our surroundings: emblems, symbols, signs, logos, jingles, and so on. Add to this our earlier discussion of sorting and saturation. The sites we ordinarily inhabit are segregated according to partisanship. More importantly, they embed partisan cues simply in virtue of being *commercial* spaces. With partisanship expanded into a lifestyle, the advertisements we encounter in day-to-day life can serve to make our political identity salient. Civic solitude requires distance from those material conditions as well.

To put the two considerations together, civic solitude calls for us to remove ourselves not only from the company of others, but also from the spaces that we most commonly occupy. This naturally raises the question of *where* we can enact civic solitude. That we might struggle with the very idea of settings that are not already claimed by partisan politics is suggestive of the magnitude of the problem we are trying to address. However, before explaining the kinds of environments that are suited to civic solitude, a few additional details must be set in place. We'll pick up the thread by looking a second kind of distance—what we called *conceptual* distance.

As was just noted, settings of isolation can be a breeding ground for the corroboration of our partisan perspectives. Think of the proverbial recluse or outsider, hunched over a computer screen, doing his "own research" about world affairs. Thinking in isolation from others provides shelter from criticism and other forms of pushback; it is associated with radicalization and unhinged conspiracy-theorizing. Civic solitude thus must come to more than retreating to insulated spaces to think about politics—this is simply a recipe for the solidification of the centered partisan self. Civic solitude hence calls for political reflection that is also at a *conceptual* distance from the predominant political idiom.

To get the sense of what this amounts to, remember that the polarization dynamic *consolidates* our lives around partisan affiliation. It thereby leads us to see everything we do as an expression our political identity, which in turn homogenizes our social relations and shrinks our perspective. We thus come to understand the world around us increasingly in terms of partisan categories and their corresponding loyalties and rivalries. Moreover, as the partisan self becomes centered, we become more *invested* in our political identity. As a result, what feels to us like critical political thinking often comes to no more than reformulating our habitual partisan scripts.

Civic solitude thus calls for a kind of *conceptual* distance. It requires self-critical political reflection that is guarded against the tendency to merely reinstate our existing partisan rivalries and affinities. So civic solitude involves political thinking that is not conducted in the vernacular current partisanship. In other words, responsible political self-criticism that aims to manage polarization must come from outside the confines of our existing political idiom.

Were it not such a cliché, one might say that civic solitude demands self-critical political thinking that goes "outside the box." But as things stand, it's better to say that decentering the partisan self requires self-critical political reflection that does not employ the familiar terms of partisan discourse. Civic solitude thus calls for political self-criticism that is conceptually detached from our routine political vocabulary, distanced from the conceptual terrain that houses our familiar partisan idiom.

4.3.2 The Practice of Atopia

A new challenge arises. We need the distance of civic solitude because our ordinary social and conceptual spaces are already colonized by forces that instigate the tendencies we must counteract. However, it is clear that political reflection in general—and arguably *critical* political thinking in particular—is at least in large part interrogative, a process of *exchanging reasons*, as philosophers say. So it seems we need political interlocutors.

Yet we have seen that when it comes to decentering, we're on our own. And, to compound this difficulty, the necessary critical reflection must be conceptually distant, it cannot be focused anticipating and responding to the pushback that is likely to come from our partisan opposition. Civic solitude is not secluded political strategizing, after all. Hence the difficulty. We need to formulate critical pushback that's not situated within our political idiom. How can we do that?

Here's the short answer: we must exercise our imagination. The more detailed answer is that we must strive to envision new kinds of interlocutors who confront us with critical perspectives that are not readily translatable into the vernacular of our usual partisanship. Decentering the partisan self requires us to imagine critical interlocutors from beyond the frontiers of our present political context.

That's easier said than done. Moreover, it might seem that the enterprise is doomed from the start. With our partisan selves centered, our cognitive and affective faculties are captured by the polarization dynamic, and this includes our *imaginative* capacities.

How are we supposed to envision critics who are not merely stand-ins for our caricatured partisan foes?

This challenge is significant, but not insurmountable. Again, the role of responsible self-critic is not a walk-on part. It takes distinctive effort. Even though we're on our own, we can nonetheless access sources of the required criticism; we can populate our imaginations with interlocutors that speak from outside of our political idiom. We do this by exposing ourselves to ideas and arguments that belong to political worlds that are not ours, and then resisting the impulse to translate them into our own context.

We might call this the practice of *atopia*, drawing on the Greek word for (roughly) "displacement." The term is not ideal, but I hope the gist is clear enough. Civic solitude calls for a style of critical political introspection in which we imaginatively position ourselves within an unfamiliar landscape, territory that encompasses possibilities that are, strictly speaking, inaccessible from our own context. Atopia thus is a reflective process by which one confronts critical perspectives that reside outside of the conceptual boundaries that structure one's political home. Through atopic engagement, we gain imaginative access to critical perspectives that do not instigate our customary partisan impulses. We confront opposing viewpoints that cannot be placed into our existing partisan categories and therefore do not prompt prefabricated responses.

4.3.2.1 "Was Aristotle a Conservative?"

To see what I mean, consider the following. I regularly teach a college course that surveys the history of political philosophy, from Aristotle to the present. And nearly every year, at least one student in the class asks whether Aristotle was a conservative. In some ways, this is a good question. It often makes for an interesting class discussion. But when the discussion is successful, it culminates in the realization that "was Aristotle a conservative?" is an inapt question.

We need not dig into the details of Aristotle's politics to see why the question is misplaced. It's enough to point out that Aristotle lived at a time before the institution of the nation-state. His political thinking hence is indexed to *cities*, small face-to-face and culturally homogeneous communities.[18] Perhaps because of this local focus, Aristotle held that politics is an extension of ethics.[19] He thought that the best political arrangements are those that cultivate virtue in those living under them. Indeed, he saw the whole *point* of politics as that of making people good.[20] As we saw in our earlier discussion, his conception of moral development involves training, and thus moral trainers. In the end, his view is that political institutions are to be evaluated according to how well they train people to be virtuous.

Aristotle again stands in sharp contrast with modern thinking. Readers will be more accustomed to approaches that focus on nation states, which are far more populous, diverse, and complex than Aristotle's cities. Moreover, we tend to think that the state exists for the purpose of making people *law-abiding* rather than *good*. That is, we say that government exists for the sake of protecting individuals and their rights. We're hence wary of the suggestion that the state should legislate morality or adopt the role of moral tutor. In our modern view, our fundamental liberty consists largely in the ability to pursue (within broad constraints) our own ideas about what makes a person good.

There are further respects in which Aristotle's political philosophy is at odds with contemporary approaches. To mention one example, Aristotle provides at least five definitions of democracy, none of which matches our modern conception.[21] And this is to say nothing about Aristotle's notorious views about the family, gender hierarchy, and slavery.[22] But we need not get bogged down in further contrasts. Our point is that there's an mistake in the question of whether Aristotle was a conservative. He wasn't. But that's not because he was a liberal or a progressive, or what have you. Rather, it's because his political theory was not born of our circumstances. It does not slot neatly into our political scene. Accordingly, the question of where Aristotle sits within our contemporary inventory of political identities is misguided. It's not clear what any answer would mean.

Still, the impulse to situate Aristotle within our own political idiom is telling. We instinctively attempt to situate new information into familiar frameworks. That's a generally a good thing, too. However, this impulse sometimes encourages the idea that the *value* of unfamiliar ideas rests with their translatability into our customary categories. In the particular case we're discussing, it is a symptom of the centeredness of partisanship to want to situate every political idea within our landscape. At its worst, this compulsion reflects an underlying assumption that our current political vocabulary is final or complete, no longer subject to revision and correction. This disposition tethers our democratic thinking to the present; it thus locks us into the political configurations and habits we must work to disrupt. As a result, the inclination to position everything within our existing political vernacular undercuts the democratic aspiration.

4.3.2.2 The Value of Atopia

In any case, Aristotle isn't a ready fit into our political categories—he's simply not speaking our political language. So when we ask what Aristotle can tell us about our democracy, the most plausible answer is "not much." Crucially, that is not to say that Aristotle's political philosophy has nothing to offer us. Indeed, in not speaking to us, Aristotle teaches us a vital lesson.

To explain, Aristotle presents us with a mode of political analysis that cannot be readily *translated* into our contemporary vernacular. In reading him, we encounter a remarkably well-reasoned line of thought that is ultimately foreign to our own intuitive ways of thinking. And that's a central benefit of engaging with him—on the most natural understanding, Aristotle confronts us with a perspective that stands in opposition to the architecture that underlies the whole of our contemporary political landscape. Accordingly, contemporary liberals and conservatives in the United States must stand in opposition to Aristotle. Figuring out precisely how one might respond to him is a valuable atopic exercise.

Despite being misguided, the question "Was Aristotle a conservative?" thus has a distinctive value. It prompts an investigation of the terms and categories that structure our current political idiom. Too often, that idiom is regarded as brutely given, a reflection of what politics simply is. In trying to engage with Aristotle from within our idiom, we can begin to notice the constraints and limitations of the terms within which we conduct our political thinking. We come to recognize that our contemporary partisan politics occupies only a small region within systematic political thought. At the same time, we discover distinctively *democratic* options that reside beyond the boundaries of our vernacular. To take one example, Aristotle presents a plausible *democratic* critique of elections; he argues that in a democracy, public offices should be filled by lottery.[23] We might reject Aristotle's reasoning and conclusion, but in doing so we cannot rely on our customary partisan reflexes. We need to think beyond them.

That's the value of atopia. Notice that this is not a strictly *historical* enterprise. The thought isn't that we can look to Aristotle for an intriguing glimpse into a past civilization that we can then contrast with our own. Nor is the point that we find in Aristotle stimulation for a kind of self-contained contemplation that one might value in itself.[24] To be sure, the worth of great literature, art, and philosophy may be bound up with opportunities to gain historical awareness or experience the intrinsic value of wonder and introspection.

But the idea here is different. Our contention is that there's value in confronting Aristotle's political thinking *as* alien to our own. Put otherwise, the idea is that there's something distinctive to be gained in seeing his ideas as *illegible* from within our contemporary political topography. More specifically, the claim is that it is important for *contemporary democratic citizens* to encounter systematic political thinking that doesn't speak to us. Engagements of that kind can drive us to see past our own circumstances.

Now, it is one thing to say that atopia is beneficial in some general way. The present claim, however, is more specific than that. It is that atopic exercises contribute to managing polarization. Let's spell that out.

As usual, is important to emphasize the personal approach to polarization management. We are not trying to devise practices that will enable us to better understand our real-world partisan opponents or to reach consensus with them. Instead, we seek to decenter the partisan self. In the first instance, this involves expanding our sense of the range of responsible political disagreement among our allies. And this is where exercises of atopia are of special use. In thinking through critical pushback from atopic sources, we bypass reflexes that instigate partisan homogenization. As a result, we expand our sense of the range of permissible variation among our allies. In short, the partisan self can be decentered by placing our partisan commitments within a broader horizon of political thought. To do that, we need to populate our imagination with critics who aren't our *partisan* opponents.

Although I've been talking specifically about Aristotle, he isn't special in this regard. The same points can be made with respect to political thought from other historical eras. For instance, one need not get too far into Mencius, Mary Wollstonecraft, or David Walker to begin to feel decidedly not at home—the categories, classifications, and concerns simply do not comply with our contemporary framework. A similar kind of atopic distance can be achieved by looking to democracies other than one's own, or even simply by reading their constitutions. Nor need the engagement be with political *texts*. Visual art, literature, poetry, architecture, film, music, and other forms of creative expression can provide material for atopic political reflection. The crucial thing for atopia is encountering material that can prompt political thinking while also *dislocating* our partisan instincts by presenting an alien— not merely *opposing*—perspective. This feeds our imagination with sources of political criticism that do not reinscribe standing partisan fissures. Accordingly, through reflective practices of atopia, we can engage in the kind of distanced political self-criticism that decenters our partisan selves.

Without putting too fine a point on it, atopia is central to the distinctive value of the Humanities. The materials taken up in these disciplines can transport us to worlds where we can only be tourists. They supply access to lives and experiences that are not only different from ours, but not readily intelligible to us. We come to inhabit, imaginatively, contexts that can be grasped only by thinking in terms that are foreign to us. Again, this makes legible to us the contingencies and limitations of our vernacular; and this sets the conditions under which we can expand our conception of permissible variation among our political allies.

I cannot here pursue this thought about the Humanities in the detail that it deserves. It is worth noticing, however, that it runs counter to a lot of current thinking about the place of the Humanities in a liberal education. According to a popular account, college courses in the Humanities are of value specifically because they can speak to us in ways that reveal new dimensions of our experience and provide us with new tools for explaining our social worlds. On this view, access to the Humanities enables us to understand ourselves better, which in turn empowers us as democratic citizens. This sensible thought is then offered as a reason for approaching the Humanities as a kind of civic training ground. We are then led to cast the value of encountering Plato, Jane Austen, or Duke Ellington exclusively in our contemporary idiom. We begin to think that when they are presented properly, these materials *speak to us*. Plato's *Republic* teaches us about the rise of contemporary authoritarians, Austen helps us to understand subtle operations of gender hierarchy, and Ellington gives us insight into the interior dynamics of oppression.

To be clear, this is all to the good. Engagement with these materials can open our minds to new ways of understanding ourselves, here and now. And that's undoubtedly important. Yet our account points to an *additional* respect in which engagement with the Humanities is vital for democratic citizens. Specifically, it calls attention to the fact that those materials can also confront us with perspectives that *do not* speak to us and *cannot* elucidate our present circumstances. And, as I suggested above, there is a distinctive democratic benefit to encounters that expand our imaginations beyond our own circumstances. Insofar as we cast the value of the Humanities strictly in terms of their ability to illuminate the present, we shortchange their democratic power.

4.3.3 Spaces of Solitude

The basic shape of civic solitude is now in view. Managing polarization calls for occasions for atopic and self-critical political reflection. That's the *kind of activity* civic solitude involves. Now we can pick up the more straightforward sense in which we need occasional *spatial* detachment. Civic solitude requires that we distance from our ordinary social surroundings because they are sorted and saturated with partisan triggers. This prompts the question of *where* we can practice civic solitude.

Recall that what is required are spaces that are free from the partisan cues and signals that saturate our ordinary environments. Although some might be able to find those conditions at home or in other typical environments, we saw in Chapter 3 that this is increasingly uncommon. Our households, workplaces, congregations, and neighborhoods have been sorted according to political identity and are immersed in partisan prompts. If one can access the necessary circumstances for civic solitude at home or in other day-to-day settings, that's a stroke of good fortune.

Civic solitude calls for spaces that are *reliably* suited to detached reflection. Yet we cannot expect citizens to build them from scratch. We must identify *existing* sites where civic solitude can be pursued, places that occasionally can be *purposed* for the necessary introspection. It's challenging to think of locations of that kind. Our social environments are already saturated. Relatedly, both our public and nonpublic spaces have increasingly become sites of commerce, inundated with advertising and commercial messaging of other kinds.[25] They are crowded with prompts that seek to mobilize group behavior. The expansion of partisan identity into a lifestyle has left us at a loss. One might conclude that there's no escaping the forces that center our partisan selves.

This conclusion is nearly correct. And that's astounding. Arguably, part of the value of a well-functioning democracy is that it enables citizens to devote their lives to things other than politics. While it is true that citizens must invest a good deal of time and effort into democracy, it nonetheless is the mark of an oppressive social order to make politics *inescapable*. Accordingly, I've argued elsewhere that responsible citizenship calls for efforts to build sites for cooperative endeavors that are not organized around politics— activities where our partisanship is not so much suppressed as beside the point.[26] In short, part of restoring democracy is a matter of sometimes doing things other than politics.

The point here is different. Although we occasionally need to do things together that are not political, we also must sometimes to do politics all by ourselves. Again, we struggle with the very idea of political engagement that is nonetheless solitary. So let's leave the "civic" part of civic solitude aside for a moment and locate familiar settings that readily lend themselves to quiet reflection.

Specifically, think of public libraries, parks, and museums. Yes, these are public spaces where multiple people tend to be present, and they are also sites of significant community engagement. But they are also sites where otherwise ordinary forms of social interaction are discouraged. They are spaces designed to permit people to be alone, quietly, with their thoughts. Notably, they are generally *noncommercial* spaces as well. Hence they also tend to be environments that are free of overt expressions of partisan identity. Except in special circumstances, they are settings where partisan displays are out of place. And in the case of libraries and museums in particular, they are sites designed to make available to us unfamiliar ideas, sentiments, and perspectives.

These are existing venues that facilitate the necessary social and conceptual distance. They thus are the most obvious places where citizens can practice civic solitude. That they don't readily spring to mind as settings for decidedly *civic* behavior is noteworthy. It is explained by the predisposition to think that democracy happens "in the streets," and thus that the civic is always collective and out in the open. Once that idea is accepted, venues that are quiet and reserved appear to us as non-civic—sites for something other than politics. Thus we tend to regard libraries, parks, and museums as places of leisure, enrichment, or recreation. We might even think of them as earmarked for socially advantaged citizens who can afford moments of idleness.

Of course, this view captures a common sentiment. Libraries, parks, and museums are frequently treated as community amenities. Judging from how public officials talk about these institutions, they are seen as optional expenditures, pleasant but superfluous indulgences. That is, these sites are regarded as extras that enhance the communities that can afford them and elect to support them. Consequently, funding for libraries, parks, and museums is always tenuous. When budgeting pressures escalate, they're easy first targets.[27]

If the foregoing argument holds, this way of thinking is profoundly misguided. Venues where citizens can escape the clamor of partisanship while also being exposed unfamiliar ideas, uncommon attitudes, and alien perspectives are *essential* for healthy democracy. Accordingly, noncommercial public sites that can foster solitary reflection are not luxuries. Rather, they're spaces for indispensable democratic practice, much on the order of public schools, municipal buildings, and polling stations. What's more, according to the view we have developed, existing disparities of access to such sites are not only lamentable products of unpleasant patterns of social disadvantage; they are also *democratic* deficiencies, ways in which society is failing to take up the democratic aspiration.

In part, it is because we are so accustomed to thinking of citizenship strictly in its collective aspects that institutions like libraries, museums, and parks have become "politicized," sites of partisan wrangling. In overemphasizing the idea that democracy happens "in the streets," we have encouraged the idea that these public institutions serve distinctively partisan objectives rather than democratic purposes. In this way, our proposal offers a *democratic* argument for free public libraries, parks, and museums. These are democratic, not merely partisan, commons. But this is not only because these sites can serve as spaces for citizens of all kinds to assemble, collaborate, and engage together in politics. The view we have developed supplies a distinctive kind of argument for regarding libraries, parks, and museums as essential to democracy: these sites provide opportunities for the kind of distanced and atopic political introspection that is necessary for responsible citizenship, but is generally unavailable to us within other social settings.

4.3.4 Is Civic Solitude Elitist?

Some will object that civic solitude is elitist. To wrap up this chapter, let's consider two versions of this charge. According to one, the proposal presupposes that citizens have the *resources* to enact civic solitude. The other objects that the proposal presupposes that citizens will have *interest* in the kind of political reflection that civic solitude involves.

We can think of the former objection as the claim that civic solitude is too *demanding* of citizens' time. People are busy. They have jobs and families, and these both call for full-time attention. Civic solitude requires free time, and that's a luxury. Accordingly, our proposal is elitist in that it identifies as a requirement of responsible citizenship an activity that most citizens cannot fully engage in. For most citizens, there simply aren't enough hours in the day.

The premises of this objection are undeniable. Free time, specifically time that is not controlled by the demands of one's employer, is increasingly scant.[28] Disparities in the social distribution of free time plausibly regarded as unjust.[29] And, moreover, the political dimensions of how the social world is organized temporally are as yet undertheorized.[30] Still, the proposed objection runs in the wrong direction. The fact that democratic citizens lack the *time* for civic solitude is not a criticism the proposal, but rather as an indictment of the broader social forces that make discretionary time so scarce. The civic solitude proposal enables us to say that prevailing conditions are unacceptable because they are incompatible with the democratic aspiration.

This brings us to the second version of the charge of elitism. It holds that civic solitude is elitist because it proposes that responsible citizenship is partly a matter of being a *scholar* of politics. The objection continues that most citizens aren't concerned with political theories. Instead, they're interested in changing the material conditions under which they live. So they don't need to learn about Aristotle. They need better access to the conditions that enable them to mobilize for political change. And, insofar as the civic solitude proposal diverts attention and effort away from concrete democratic action, it favors the status quo and obstructs change. The status quo unacceptably benefits those who belong to a small class of social and economic elites. For that reason, civic solitude is elitist.

This is a more formidable criticism than the first. Yet it, too, is misplaced. For one thing, the presumed opposition between democratic action and democratic theorizing is overplayed. As anyone who has engaged in political activism knows well, the task is driven by ideas. Coalition-building, organizing, and mobilization depend in large part on the successful articulation of political objectives and priorities. These are unavoidably formulated in the language of political theory, broadly understood. In fact, the dominant political movements of our day are organized around the conceptual materials of the political philosopher: liberty, fascism, socialism, accountability, inclusion, national identity, the rule of law, insurrection, abuse of power, immunity, and so on.

Of course, in popular political discourse these terms are derelict. They are used in catchphrases, slogans, and slurs—they do not function as political *ideas* so much as strictly rhetorical tokens of one's partisan identity. That's correct. But, again, that's the problem that civic solitude is meant to address. No matter how activism-oriented one's view of politics might be, the business of democracy is conducted in the language of ideas. Building a viable social movement is for this reason partly a theoretical endeavor. It takes clear thinking about aims, options, and possibilities. We have surveyed a range of considerations suggesting that our political thinking is easily hijacked by cognitive and affective dynamics that are activated in group settings. In this way, civic solitude is proposed as a strategy for cultivating the capacities that enable us to be more astute in our democratic thinking, and thus more responsible in our political advocacy.

Civic solitude is therefore not elitist in the envisioned sense. It does not seek to displace political energies that otherwise would be deployed towards activism, and does not impede political change. Instead, it seeks to disrupt patterns of political mobilization that are unthinking, reactionary, and merely impulsive, given the centrality of our partisan selves. To aim for a citizenry that's less susceptible to inflammatory rhetoric and provocative appeals to tribal identities is not elitist. And neither is the argumentative path that leads to the suggestion that the pursuit of this aim calls for occasions for solitary and detached political contemplation.

A more general point is worth making. Anyone who thinks that democracy requires more of us than the physical act of casting a ballot on Election Day is thereby invested in a view of responsible citizenship that imposes significant demands on ordinary people.

Familiar proposals that citizens must contribute to the life of their democracy—whether by activism, deliberation, volunteerism, or other modes of community involvement—all invoke claims on our time, attention, and energy. As noted above, access to the necessary material, social, and psychological resources is bound to be unevenly distributed across the citizenry. And in many cases, these inequalities will track patterns of unjust social advantage. Accordingly, they will be sites of injustice in their own right.

We might say that democracy is in this respect *tragic*.[31] On nearly any plausible interpretation of the idea of self-government among equals, democracy calls for citizens to engage in political activities beyond the voting booth. However, as we expand our inventory of the requirements of authentic democracy, we also create new sites of democratic malfunction. To illustrate, consider that on any robust view of our civic responsibilities, citizens will be required to draw on their personal resources. And these resources are unequally distributed. In some cases, these inequalities are inevitable and perhaps for that reason unobjectionable. For instance, some citizens simply do not have the *temperament* for protracted civic engagement. However, other disparities have to do with inequitable *access* to the channels of democratic involvement.

As we noted a moment ago, democratic engagement takes time, effort, attention, energy. It thus imposes opportunity costs—resources devoted to politics are thus not available for other uses. These inequalities in access will tend to favor those who already enjoy various other forms of social and economic advantage. That is, those who are already materially secure enjoy far greater access to the sites and processes of democratic decision-making and social change. As a result, these disparities result in corresponding differences in political influence.

Thus the tragedy. In an effort to make society more genuinely democratic, we wind up reinforcing existing patterns of social advantage and disadvantage. More than that, we construct new sites where social advantage can be leveraged into political influence.

These unwelcome byproducts of our efforts to enhance the authenticity of our democracy are often nevertheless unavoidable.

I raise this tragic feature of democracy not because I believe that civic solitude can resolve it. Rather, the point is that it must be confronted by *any* view of democracy that embraces a normative conception of citizenship. In this way, any robust vision of responsible democratic citizenship is subject to the charge of elitism. If civic solitude is objectionably elitist, then so is any view that asks citizens to do more than cast a vote on Election Day.

4.4 Conclusion

The book's central argument is complete. It now can be stated succinctly. In order to thrive, democracy needs citizens to be both politically active and politically reflective. Yet in their activity and their reflection, citizens must recognize the political equality of their fellow citizens. Thus, responsible democratic citizenship invokes an ethos of civility, modes of political advocacy that are attuned to the concerns, values, and perspectives of one's fellow citizens. The trouble is that these very modes of political engagement subject us to the polarization dynamic, an assembly of forces that impair the cognitive and affective capacities required for civility. Democracy, in this sense, is subject to an autoimmune disorder.

As it arises from within the office of democratic citizenship, this disorder cannot be eradicated, but only managed. And for the same reason, it cannot be addressed from within our usual civic practices. To manage polarization, we need to do something new. In addition to civility, we must also introduce practices aimed at polarization management.

Given the nature of the problem of polarization, the management task is a matter of dislodging partisanship as our central mode of social identity. Our prescription thus is for democratic citizens to seek out occasions for atopic and self-critical political introspection.

Although public spaces in general tend to be unsuited to this kind of reflection, there nonetheless are existing sites where citizens can pursue civic solitude. Specifically, public libraries, parks, and museums are places that already lend themselves to civic solitude. For this reason, they are democratically essential venues precisely because they can enable detached reflection. Insofar as society permits severe disparities in access to sites of this kind, it is failing at democracy.

Similarly, to the extent that citizens are fixated on the urgencies of politics and therefore disposed to dismiss the civic value of solitary political reflection, they too are failing at democracy. Yes, democracy happens when citizens take to the streets together to hold government to account. But that's not democracy's only locus. And it might not be democracy's most important site. Democracy also can occur when a citizen, sitting alone, opens a book, watches a film, studies a painting, or simply encounters an idea that transports them into a distant mode of political thinking that does not speak to their own circumstances.

Epilogue

Democracy—The Task Within Us

Imagine *Panopolis*, a modern democratic society much like our own. Like many contemporary democracies, Panopolian politics is configured around two broad camps. To keep things simple, let's stipulate that even though there are no legal prohibitions on forming political parties of other kinds, Panopolian politics is dominated by its two major parties: the Liberal Party, and the Conservative Party. Of course, citizens recognize that there are variations *within* each camp. For example, they understand that some Liberal Party affiliates are more *progressive* than others, while some Conservative Party members are more *traditional* than average. Nonetheless, Panopolian citizens tend overwhelmingly to affiliate with one of the two major parties.

So far, Panopolis might look familiar. What makes it distinctive is that it is a society organized *entirely* around politics.

The first thing to note is that Panopolis is partitioned into geographical regions designated by partisan allegiance. In each district, the shopping centers, entertainment venues, religious institutions, schools, workplaces, restaurants, and recreational facilities all reflect the political commitments of the citizens who reside within. Accordingly, in Panopolis' liberal precincts, one finds neighborhoods with sidewalks and plenty of apartment housing, electric-car-charging stations, locally owned shops selling organic food and fair-trade goods, a broad variety of yoga studios and ethnic restaurants, cinemas showing foreign-language films, and many public parks and communal gardens. Liberal districts additionally feature efficiently organized recycling programs, a variety of volunteer organizations, and robust local zoning regulations governing the use of common space.

In the conservative sectors of Panopolis, families tend to be larger, so most reside in houses on large lots with sizeable backyards. For similar reasons, they drive larger vehicles and have little use for hybrid cars. Regulations tend to protect citizens' privacy, independence, and freedom of choice. Further, conservative Panopolians tend to be more religiously devout than their liberal counterparts, and they embrace a norm of religious toleration. Their districts are thus home to a broad variety of religious institutions, places of worship, and faith-based charity organizations. At the same time, they recognize a tight connection between their religious convictions and their social and political responsibilities. Accordingly, they tend to donate generously to religious charity organizations and to volunteer within their faith community.

For similar reasons, conservative areas within Panopolis feature a high concentration of expressions of patriotism. For example, they fly the Panopolian flag with greater regularity than those who inhabit liberal neighborhoods. Conservative citizens also enjoy distinctive recreational activities. Whereas liberal Panopolians like to hike, birdwatch, travel, and lounge on a beach, conservatives enjoy golfing, fishing, hunting, swimming in the family's own pool.

Although Panopolis is thoroughly segregated according to partisan identity, no citizen is *coerced* into these modes of living. Panopolis recognizes the freedom of association. So citizens are permitted to live and work anywhere they like within Panopolis. There are no formal barriers to entry or exit across the different sectors, and no official requirements for taking up residence or employment within a particular neighborhood. Still, there is little movement between the different kinds of district. Panopolis remains partitioned mainly because the citizens *embrace* this arrangement. They *prefer* to live, work, and socialize with their partisan allies, and are content to peacefully coexist at a distance from the political opposition.

In fact, the Panopolians see their participation in this system of geographical segregation as the *fulfillment* of their political ideals. They demand that their social environments reflect their partisan values. They insist that their day-to-day activities—from shopping and commuting to vacationing and volunteering—should express their political commitments. To them, it all feels like authenticity and, indeed, freedom.

Yet Panopolis is a single nation, governed by a common set of institutions. It is a democracy in that its major political offices are filled by way of fair and open elections with full adult suffrage. Moreover, Panopolis is ruled by laws and governed according to a public constitution. There are robust protections of individual rights. The typical political liberties are reliably preserved. There are sturdy traditions of free speech, freedom of the press, protected dissent, and peaceful transitions of power.

Accordingly, Panoplian democracy is largely a matter of *mobilization*. Candidates for political office have little need to convince citizens of their fitness for public service; nor need they try to change the minds of those citizens who are not already disposed to support them. The key to winning Panoplian elections is rallying the base and getting out the vote. Once elected, officials reliably work to legislate in accordance with their party's agenda, while also striving to gain reelection.

Panopolis is relatively stable. Although the two major political camps routinely disparage each other, they find ways to cooperate and compromise when absolutely necessary. They tend to see government as a kind of power-sharing among counteracting forces. Although each party wants full control of government, they're willing to settle for balance.

Overall, we could say that Panopolis is alive with politics. Indeed, given their social geography, everyone in Panopolis is constantly enacting their democratic commitments. With every purchase, every walk around the neighborhood, and every round of golf, Panopolians are living their partisanship. They are perpetually *participating* in politics. And because their participation places them in contact nearly exclusively with their co-partisans, their daily activities fortify their social bonds. Accordingly, social trust, empathy, and feelings of solidarity are especially high—among co-partisans at least. In some ways, Panopolis may seem a democratic utopia.

Yet not all is well within Panopolis. From the perspective developed in this book, Panopolis is failing at democracy. For one thing, Panopolians are not really living together as democratic equals. They are merely living *alongside* each other. That they are managing to do so peacefully is remarkable.

In fact, the envisioned stability of Panopolis strains the imagination. This is because Panopolian citizens live under conditions that heighten their exposure to the forces that drive the polarization dynamic. If Panopolis is a peaceful society, it won't stay that way for long. Eventually the dispositions that allow for peaceful co-existence with partisan opposition will give way to tendencies that regard political rivals as incompetent, depraved, and threatening. Panopolians will come to see those who live outside of their own sectors as social aliens who are divested from democracy. The practice of living peaceably under a common set of governing institutions will eventually fall away. Power-sharing in government will start to feel like capitulation, and thus self-betrayal. In short, Panopolis is doomed.

We do not live in Panopolis. However, we have reviewed several respects in which our democracy is more like Panopolis than we might have expected. Not only are our everyday environments sorted according to partisan affiliation and saturated with partisan cues, *we* are similar to the Panopolians. Like them, we are disposed to see democracy as fundamentally a matter of collective political action. We accordingly laud political participation as such—at least when the participant is on our side. For us, as for Panopolians, democratic politics is centrally about large-scale *mobilization*. Again, on a popular view of these matters, that's what democracy looks like.

I cannot emphasize enough that, indeed, democracy *does* look like that. Yet, as was argued at the start of this book, images of mass political action strike us as paradigmatically democratic only if we make certain assumptions about the participants. They must not be paid actors, they must be adequately informed, they must be moved by certain aims, and so on. This is enough to set in motion the central idea of this book. While it is true that democracy is a collective endeavor that requires citizens to engage in coordinated public action, it is also—and perhaps more fundamentally—a matter of what goes on inside each of us when we take up our civic role.

The interior aspects of citizenship are all the more crucial once we recognize that the familiar *external* manifestations of democracy can corrupt our civic capacities. To repeat, this is true even in the case of otherwise *responsible* democratic activities. This means that it's not enough to stand up for the right policies or to embrace the correct political stance. As important as it might be for a democracy to enact good laws and policies, that's not all there is to democracy's health. What matters for responsible democratic citizenship is what lies *beneath* your political posture—how you *arrived* at your perspective, and what sensibilities you bring to your public advocacy.

The lesson of our analysis of the polarization dynamic is that we are not good judges of these matters. We cannot see our political selves clearly, and thus cannot reliably gauge the democratic quality of our own attitudes. This is because we are subject to stealthy forces that distort our political judgment. Accordingly, insofar as we are truly invested in the democratic aspiration, we need to embrace practices that can mitigate that distortion. According to the argument developed here, this calls for civic solitude.

Although civic solitude consists in distanced thinking, it nonetheless imposes burdens. For those who are especially politically active, it means taking time away from favorite projects and ordinary social interactions. When we're in the throes of politics, any digression away from the cause is bound to feel like a setback. In some cases, civic solitude will draw energies away from the pursuit of our more immediate political aims. Civic solitude sometimes feels like political retreat.

Yet we need to remember that democracy is a long game. The project of building a society that more faithfully realizes a self-governing society of equals does not belong only to us, in the here and now. It is also the future-oriented endeavor of cultivating the social conditions under which democracy can more fully thrive. Accordingly, our civic task is not only that of achieving the best collective decision or policy outcome. It is rather that of promoting the cause of social justice *while also* advancing the democratic aspiration. This means that in seeking to promote justice, we must not lose sight of the fact that our fellow citizens, including those who embrace political ideas that conflict with our own, are our equals. Getting the right policy outcome by means that disregard the equality of our fellow citizens is an overall democratic loss, an instance of subordinating others to your own will.

In addition to that, we must recognize that the vocabulary of our politics—the idiom within which we understand and articulate our partisan loyalties, commitments, and rivalries—is an artifact of our political past. In many respects, it is the product of the social forces that we must try to counteract. Pursuing the democratic ideal thus involves welcoming—and perhaps provoking—periodic conceptual renovations. Such transformation is necessary if we are to break out of our old routines of partisanship and learn new democratic habits. In other words, we give up on the democratic aspiration insofar as we commit ourselves to reproducing our political present. But that's exactly how our standing political vernacular functions; it locks us into a network of loyalties and rivalries that doom us to a democratic future that replicates our past.

In short, democracy calls for us to see beyond ourselves. It requires the recognition that the endeavor is not all about us. So we must not allow the democratic horizon to be captured by our current partisan rivalries and the policy challenges that aggravate them. To be sure, seeing beyond our partisan selves is not easy. Their characteristic scripts and reflexes are inscribed into our self-understandings. The task involves the exertion of our political imagination to the point where we might catch a glimpse of a democratic future that is profoundly unlike our present, because it is organized around patterns of political identity that are not fully legible from where we stand.

The project of imagining that kind of future starts small. It begins with individual acts of civic introspection, exercises that help us to see the problem of our toxic politics as partly *our* problem. Importantly, this does not mean seeing it as a problem with our cross-partisan relations. Rather, the crucial realization is that political toxicity has its origins in our own civic dispositions, what *we* bring to democracy. This clears the ground for the recognition that responsible democratic citizenship is a project of internal investigation, regulation, and maintenance. It allows us to see that although the democratic enterprise is largely that of building collectively toward a self-governing political order that is more authentically a society of equals, it is also an individual project—a task within each of us.

If you live in the United States, there's a good chance that a Google Images search for the phrase "this is what democracy looks like" will return many photographs taken on the National Mall in Washington, DC. Centrally located in the capital city and surrounded by iconic monuments and the central sites of government power, the National Mall provides a fitting setting for large-scale political engagement. Amid the Washington Monument, the Lincoln Memorial, the Capitol Building, and the White House—it's hard to imagine a better place for democracy to get done.

Yet the National Mall is also a public park. It features several relatively secluded lawns and walking paths the provide access to public sculptures. It is bordered by museums. And although it is easy to overlook in the images delivered in the Google search, central to the space is the Lincoln Memorial Reflecting Pool. When visiting the National Mall, it takes effort to escape the commotion of tour groups and government employees going about their ordinary business. But even when the area is busy, it is possible to find a quiet spot to sit at the edge of the Reflecting Pool. The central claim of this book has been that a distinctive and crucial part of the work of democracy can happen there, too.

Notes

Chapter 1

1. For a sample, consult Caplan 2007; Somin 2013; Brennan 2016; Achen and Bartels 2016; and Freiman 2020.
2. In May of 2023, the US Surgeon General issued a report referring to loneliness and isolation as an "epidemic" (US Surgeon General 2023). For a discussion of the dangers of social disconnection, see Brownlee 2020.
3. See also Green 2015.
4. Bail et al. 2018.
5. Claassen and Ensley 2016.
6. Sunstein 2017. See also Vaidhyanathan 2018.

Chapter 2

1. Anderson 2021; Hannon 2021.
2. It is not surprising that we have a term for this mode of democratic forgery: "astroturfing." The term conveys the idea that *authentic* democratic action is grown from the roots up rather than imposed from above.
3. Of the latter, some hold that although citizens *taken individually* are generally incompetent, citizens assembled in properly structured *groups* can be not only competent, but even wise. See Landemore 2012 and 2020.
4. We can set aside the complication that democratic citizens sometimes also vote on referendum questions, which decide policy more or less directly. We also do not need to examine the extra-electoral channels by which democratic citizens might contribute to self-rule, such as certain kinds of community organizing. Nothing hangs on these matters at present.
5. However, Landemore (2020), Lopez-Guerra (2011), and Guerrero (2014) defend non-electoral forms of democracy. See Lafont 2020 for criticism.
6. I am referring to what is called *philosophical* anarchism (Wolf 1970; Simmons 1980). Philosophical anarchism is strictly the view that no political order is normatively justified. This is different from what is sometimes

called "bottles and bricks" anarchism, which holds that that all states must be eliminated. Philosophical anarchism does not entail the bottles-and-bricks version, as the morally unjustified *status quo* could be morally preferable overall to the most likely outcome of destroying existing states.
7. I'm here using the term *aristocracy* in the literal sense: the rule of the best. Classical forms of monarchism are thus aristocratic.
8. On popular readings, Plato, Rousseau, Hegel, and Marx are social holists. In the 1980s and 1990s, there was a movement in political theory that called itself "communitarianism," which embraced some elements of social holism, but also claimed to be democratic (see Sandel 1982). Discussion of these views would take us too far afield.
9. See Kolodny 2023 for a comprehensive elaboration of this idea.
10. Philosophers disagree about what *accounts for* our equal standing. Thankfully, we need not delve into that debate here. Our concern lies not with the justification of the claim that we are equals, but with its implications. Be assured that the elucidation I have provided reflects the common ground among the conflicting views of what makes us equals.
11. This formulation is due to Waldron 2017.
12. This is not to deny that the failure to satisfy certain responsibilities of citizenship can *wrong* our fellow citizens. For example, profoundly biased jurors can wrong criminal defendants. And those who refuse to sit for jury duty wrong their fellow citizens in ways that can be criminal. But these issues lie beyond our present concerns.
13. See Bejan 2017; Keith and Danisch 2020; Zamalin 2021; Hudson 2023.
14. Pettit 2012: 84.
15. This is the central theme of Talisse 2021.
16. Williams 1973: 116.
17. MacIntyre 1981: 188.

Chapter 3

1. Saad 2023: https://news.gallup.com/poll/508169/historically-low-faith-institutions-continues.aspx.
2. Harvard Youth poll 2023: https://iop.harvard.edu/youth-poll/45th-edition-spring-2023
3. Pew 2021: https://www.pewresearch.org/short-reads/2021/11/23/republicans-and-democrats-alike-say-its-stressful-to-talk-politics-with-people-who-disagree/.

4. Pew 2019a: https://www.pewresearch.org/short-reads/2019/07/18/americans-say-the-nations-political-debate-has-grown-more-toxic-and-heated-rhetoric-could-lead-to-violence/.
5. Pew 2023: https://www.pewresearch.org/politics/2023/06/21/inflation-health-costs-partisan-cooperation-among-the-nations-top-problems/. Pew 2019b: https://www.pewresearch.org/politics/2014/06/12/section-4-political-compromise-and-divisive-policy-debates/.
6. https://www.monmouth.edu/polling-institute/reports/monmouthpoll_US_062023/.
7. Shepard 2023: https://www.politico.com/news/2023/03/31/donald-trump-indictment-00090001.
8. EIU 2021: https://www.eiu.com/n/campaigns/democracy-index-2021/.
9. *Global State of Democracy 2021*: 8; *Global State of Democracy 2022*: 31; *Global State of Democracy 2023*: 131.
10. EIU Democracy Index 2021: 55; International IDEA *Global State of Democracy* 2022: 28; International IDEA *Global State of Democracy* 2023: 74.
11. https://www.theguardian.com/us-news/2021/nov/22/us-list-backsliding-democracies-civil-liberties-international.
12. Klein 2020: xix.
13. In the *New York Times*, Thomas Edsell warns that polarization may have reached a "point of no return" (Edsell 2021). In *The New Yorker*, Elizabeth Kolbert asks "how did politics get so polarized?" (Kolbert 2022).
14. On the twentieth anniversary of the 9/11 attacks, G. W. Bush lamented the "malign force" that "turns every disagreement into an argument, and every argument into a clash of cultures" (Bush 2021). In an op-ed about the January 6 Insurrection, Jimmy Carter urged Americans to "resist the polarization that is reshaping our identities around politics" (Carter 2022). In his Inaugural, Biden called repeatedly for "unity" (Biden 2021).
15. Compare Rawls on the "fact of oppression" (2005: 36f.).
16. The following account updates the discussion in Talisse 2021.
17. See Fiorina, Abrams, and Pope 2005; Abramowitz and Saunders 2008; and Hetherington, Long, and Rudolph 2016.
18. See Levendusky 2009.
19. In the United States, the terms "RINO" ("Republican in name only") and "neoliberal" (a professed liberal who nonetheless endorses markets) serve this purpose.
20. See Abramowitz and Saunders 2008; Fiorina and Abrams 2008.
21. Iyengar and Krupenkin 2018.

22. See Iyengar, Lelkes, Levendusky, Malhotra, and Westwood 2019 for a review. See also Druckman and Levendusky 2019.
23. Druckman and Levendusky 2019: 115.
24. There's a debate over whether affective polarization is symmetrical across the partisan divide between Democrats and Republicans. The data are mixed. See Jost, van der Linden, Panagopoulos, and Hardin 2018 for results suggesting that affective polarization is more prevalent among conservatives. See Iyengar, Lelkes, Levendusky, Malhotra, and Westwood 2019 for data suggesting symmetrical affective polarization.
25. Levendusky and Malhorta 2016; Mason 2018b; and Dias and Lelkes 2022.
26. Here it is important to stress that we are talking about *citizens'* policy commitments, not the expressed commitments of the major political parties or their officials. See Iyengar and Krupenkin 2018, and Mason 2018a: 73.
27. Kalmoe and Mason 2022: 47.
28. Kalmoe and Mason 2019: 22. See also Edsell, "No Hate Left Behind," *New York Times*.
29. Iyengar, Sood, and Lelkes 2012.
30. McConnell et al. 2017; Hetherington and Weiler 2018.
31. Iyengar and Westwood 2015: 691.
32. Huber and Malhotra 2017; Iyengar and Konitzer 2017.
33. Nicholson, Coe, Emory, and Song 2016.
34. Bougher 2017.
35. Moore-Berg, Hameiri, and Bruneau, 2020.
36. Ahler 2014; Alher and Sood 2018; Druckman et al. 2022.
37. See More in Common: https://perceptiongap.us/. See also Beyond Conflict: https://beyondconflictint.org/americas-divided-mind/
38. Jenke 2023; Wang, et al. 2023.
39. Mason 2018a: 70ff.
40. Achen and Bartels 2016: 307f.
41. Hannon 2022.
42. More precisely, affective polarization can help us understand heightened *expressions* of platform and elite polarization. In the United States, the parties and party members are not as divided over political policies as they present themselves as being.
43. Lee 2016.
44. Iyengar and Krupenkin 2018: 215; Groenendky and Banks 2014; Valentino et al. 2011.
45. Wagner 2021.

46. The phenomenon is sometimes called "group polarization." Here, this more common name is misleading. I am distinguishing political polarization and belief polarization, and both have to do with groups.
47. Moscovici and Zavalloni 1969.
48. Myers and Bishop 1970.
49. Myers 1975.
50. Hastie, Schkade, and Sunstein 2007.
51. Baron et al. 1996: 548.
52. Turner et al. 1987: 153.
53. Turner et al. 1987: 153.
54. The Appendix in Sunstein 2009 catalogues the experimental results.
55. Hence Lamm and Myers (1978: 146), "Seldom in the history of social psychology has a nonobvious phenomenon been so firmly grounded in data from across a variety of cultures and dependent measures."
56. Taber and Lodge 2006.
57. Gaertner et al. 1993.
58. Westfall et al. 2015; Sunstein 2009: 44.
59. Stoner 1968.
60. Sunstein 2019: 84.
61. Hogg 2001.
62. Lee 2021.
63. Mason 2018a: 14; Hetherington and Weiler 2018: 17.
64. Marques et al. 1988.
65. Myers et al. 1980.
66. Lamm and Myers 1978: 185.
67. Baron et al. 1996.
68. Abrams et al. 1990; Lee 2007.
69. Van Swol 2009: 194.
70. Hogg 2001.
71. Baron et al. 1996: 558.
72. Baron et al. 1996: 559.
73. West and Iyengar 2020.
74. Mason and Wronski 2018.
75. Westwood, Iyengar, Walgrave, Leonisio, Miller, and Strijbis 2017; Iyengar and Krupenkin 2018.
76. Bishop 2009. See also Kaplan, Spenkuch, and Sullivan 2022.
77. Chen and Rodden 2013; Tam et al. 2013.
78. Iyengar, Konitzer, and Tedin 2018
79. Stoker and Jennings 1995; Hetherington and Weiler 2018: 93.

80. Hetherington and Weiler 2018: 94.
81. Klofstad, McDermott, and Hatemi 2013; Hetherington and Weiler 2018: 93ff.
82. Pew 2014
83. Brown and Enos 2021.
84. Mutz and Mondak 2006; Bonica, Chilton, and Sen 2015; Iyengar and Westwood 2015; Mason 2015; Margolis 2018.
85. Carney, Jost, Gosling, and Potter 2008.
86. McConnell, Margalit, Malhorta, and Levendusky 2017.
87. Mason 2018a: 43.
88. Gerber and Huber 2009; Hetherington and Weiler 2018: 100ff.
89. Hetherington and Weiler 2018: 91.
90. Layman and Carsey 2002; Cohen 2003; Achen and Bartels 2016: 234; Mason 2018a: 74; Van Bavel et al. 2024.
91. Brader and Tucker 2018.
92. Putnam 1995.
93. Mason and Wronski 2018.
94. Lee 2021; Shafranek 2020.
95. Coffey and Joseph 2013; Margolis and Sances 2017; Rawlings and Childress 2023.
96. DellaPosta, Shi, and Macy 2015.
97. Benson 2023
98. Iyengar and Krupenkin 2018: 34.
99. Joshi 2020.
100. Kalmoe and Mason 2022.
101. Bail et al. 2018.
102. Nyhan and Reifler 2010.
103. Jenke 2023; Bisgaard 2019.
104. Ditto et al. 2019; Nyhan 2020.
105. See Talisse 2021: 97ff.
106. Puglisi and Snyder 2011; Sood and Iyengar 2016.
107. Wagner 2021.
108. Lee 2016.
109. Martin and Nai 2024.

Chapter 4

1. Dewey 1939.
2. Hannon 2022.

3. See Curato et al. 2017 for an overview.
4. See, for example, Fishkin 2018; Landemore 2020; Guerrero 2014.
5. Aristotle 1962: 1105b5.
6. Aristotle 1962: 1103b30.
7. Aristotle 1962: 1103b1.
8. Braver Angels, "The Numbers are In" (2023): https://braverangels.org/the-numbers-are-in/.
9. Mendelberg 2002.
10. Hastie, Schkade, and Sunstein 2007; Bail et al. 2018.
11. Mutz 2006; Mutz 2013.
12. Voelkel et al. 2023.
13. Thomsen and Thomsen 2022; Wojcieszak and Warner 2020.
14. See Christensen et al. 2016 and Santoro and Brockman 2022. See also Neblo et al. 2010.
15. Cherry 2021.
16. Benson 2023.
17. Some research suggests that norms of self-critique within a group tend make the members more open toward outsiders, while also improving outsiders' dispositions toward the group. See Saguy and Halperin 2014.
18. Aristotle 1997: 1252a6.
19. Aristotle 1962: 1179b31.
20. Aristotle 1997: 1252b28.
21. Aristotle 1997: 1291b30ff.
22. Aristotle 1997: 1252a24f; 1253b23f.
23. Aristotle 1997: 1294a30ff.
24. See Hitz 2020 for a defense of thinking for its own sake.
25. See, for example, Enos 2017; Parkinson 2012; and the articles collected in Law and Smith 2006.
26. Talisse 2019.
27. Peet 2022; Cineas 2023. See also Barclay 2017.
28. Anderson 2017.
29. Rose 2016.
30. Cohen 2018 is a notable exception.
31. Elliott raises a related point, what he calls the "paradox of empowerment" (2023: 72ff.).

Works Cited

Abramowitz, A. I., and K. L. Saunders. 2008. "Is Polarization a Myth?" *The Journal of Politics* 70.2: 542–555.
Abrams, D., M. Wetherell, S. Cochrane, M. A. Hogg, and J. C. Turner. 1990. "Knowing What to Think by Knowing Who You Are: Self-categorization and the Nature of Norm Formation, Conformity and Group Polarization." *British Journal of Social Psychology* 29.2: 97–119.
Achen, Christopher H., and Larry M. Bartels. 2016. *Democracy for Realists: Why Elections Do Not Produce Responsive Government.* Princeton, NJ: Princeton University Press.
Ahler, Douglas J. 2014. "Self-Fulfilling Misperceptions of Public Polarization." *Journal of Politics* 76: 607–620.
Ahler, Douglas J., and Guarav Sood. 2018. "The Parties in Our Heads: Misperception about Party Composition and their Consequences." *Journal of Politics* 80: 964–981.
Anderson, Elizabeth. 2017. *Private Government.* Princeton, NJ: Princeton University Press.
Anderson, Elizabeth. 2021. "Epistemic Bubbles and Authoritarian Politics." In Elizabeth Edenberg and Michael Hannon, eds. *Political Epistemology*, 11–30. New York: Oxford University Press.
Aristotle. 1962. *Nicomchean Ethics.* Martin Ostwald, translator. New York: Pearson.
Aristotle. 1997. *The Politics of Aristotle.* Peter Philips Simpson, translator. Chapel Hill: University of North Carolina Press.
Bail, Christopher A., Lisa P. Argyle, Taylor W. Brown, John P. Bumpus, Haohan Chen, M. B. Fallin Hunzaker, Jaemin Lee, Marcus Mann, Friedolin Merhout, and Alexander Volfovsky. 2018. "Exposure to Opposing Views on Social Media can Increase Political Polarization." *Proceedings of the National Academy of Sciences* 115.37: 9216–9221.
Barclay, Donald. 2017. "Space and the Social Worth of Public Libraries." *Public Library Quarterly* 36.4: 267–273.
Baron, Robert S., Sieg I. Hoppe, Chaun Feng Kao, Bethany Brunsman, Barbara Linneweh, and Diana Rogers. 1996. "Social Corroboration and Opinion Extremity." *Journal of Experimental Social Psychology* 32: 537–560.
Bejan, Teresa. 2017. *Mere Civility.* Cambridge, MA: Harvard University Press.
Benson, Jonathan. 2023. "Democracy and the Epistemic Problems of Political Polarization." *American Political Science Review.* online first.

Beyond Conflict. 2020. *America's Divided Mind*. https://beyondconflictint.org/americas-divided-mind/.

Biden, Joe. 2021. "Inaugural Speech." https://www.whitehouse.gov/briefing-room/speeches-remarks/2021/01/20/inaugural-address-by-president-joseph-r-biden-jr/.

Bisgaard, Martin. 2019. "How Getting the Facts Right Can Fuel Partisan-Motivated Reasoning." *American Journal of Political Science* 63.4: 824–839.

Bishop, Bill. 2009. *The Big Sort*. New York: Harcourt Publishing.

Bonica, Adam, Adam Chilton, and Maya Sen. 2015. "The Political Ideologies of American Lawyers." *Journal of Legal Analysis* 8.2: 277–335.

Bougher, Lori D. 2017. "The Correlates of Discord: Identity, Issue Alignment, and Political Hostility in Polarized America." *Political Behavior* 39: 731–762.

Brader, Ted, and Joshua Tucker. 2018. "Unreflective Partisans? Policy Information and Evaluation in the Development of Partisanship." *Political Psychology* 39.1: 137–157.

Braver Angels. 2023. "The Numbers Are In." https://braverangels.org/the-numbers-are-in/.

Brennan, Jason. 2016. *Against Democracy*. Princeton, NJ: Princeton University Press.

Brown, J. R., and Ryan D. Enos. 2021. "The Measurement of Partisan Sorting for 180 Million Voters." *Nature Human Behaviour* 5.8: 998–1008.

Brownlee, Kimberly. 2020. *Being Sure of Each Other*. New York: Oxford University Press.

Bush, G. W. 2021. "9/11 Memorial Speech." https://www.cnn.com/2021/09/11/politics/transcript-george-w-bush-speech-09-11-2021/index.html.

Caplan, Bryan. 2007. *The Myth of the Rational Voter*. Princeton, NJ: Princeton University Press.

Carney, D. R., John T. Jost, Samuel Gosling, and Jeff Potter. 2008. "The Secret Lives of Liberals and Conservatives: Personality Profiles, Interaction Styles, and the Things They Leave Behind." *Political Psychology* 29.6: 807–840.

Carter, Jimmy. 2022. "I Fear for Our Democracy." *The New York Times*, January 5.

Chen, Jowei, and Jonathan Rodden. 2013. "Unintentional Gerrymandering: Political Geography and Electoral Bias in Legislatures." *Quarterly Journal of Political Science* 8: 239–269.

Cherry, Myisha. 2021. *The Case for Rage*. New York: Oxford University Press.

Christensen, Henrik Serup, Staffan Himmelroos, and Kimmo Grönlund. 2016. "Does Deliberation Breed an Appetite for Discursive Participation? Assessing the Impact of First-Hand Experience." *Political Studies* 65: 64–83.

Cineas, Fabiola. 2023. "The Rising Republican Movement to Defund Libraries." https://www.vox.com/politics/2023/5/5/23711417/republicans-want-to-defund-public-libraries-book-bans.

WORKS CITED

Claassen, Ryan L., and Michael Ensley. 2016. "Motivated Reasoning and Yard-Sign Stealing Partisans: Mine Is a Likeable Rogue, Yours Is a Degenerate Criminal." *Political Behavior* 38: 317–335.

Coffey, D. J., and Particia H. Joseph. 2013. "A Polarized Environment: The Effect of Partisanship and Ideological Values on Individual Recycling and Conservation Behavior." *American Behavioral Scientist* 57.1: 116–139.

Cohen, Elizabeth. 2018. *The Political Value of Time*. Cambridge: Cambridge University Press.

Cohen, Geoffrey L. 2003. "Party Over Policy: The Dominating Impact of Group Influence on Political Beliefs." *Journal of Personality and Social Psychology* 85.5: 808–822.

Curato, Nicole, John S. Dryzek, Selen A. Ercan, Carolyn M. Hendricks, and Simon Niemeyer. 2017. "Twelve Key Findings in Deliberative Democracy Research." *Daedalus* 146.3: 28–38.

DellaPosta, Daniel, Yongren Shi, and Michael Macy. 2015. "Why Do Liberals Drink Lattes?" *American Journal of Sociology* 120.5: 1473–1511.

Dewey, John 1939. "Creative Democracy—The Task Before Us." In Jo Ann Boydston, ed. *The Collected Works Of John Dewey: The Later Works*, vol. 13, 224–230. Carbondale: University of Southern Illinois Press.

Dias, Nicholas, and Y. Lelkes. 2022. "The Nature of Affective Polarization: Disentangling Policy Disagreement from Partisan Identity." *American Journal of Political Science* 66.3: 775–790.

Ditto, Peter H., Brittany Liu, Cory Clark, Sean Wojcik, Eric Chen, Rebecca Grady, Jared Celniker, and Joanne Zinger. 2019. "At Least Bias Is Bipartisan: A Meta-Analytic Comparison of Partisan Bias in Liberals and Conservatives." *Perspectives on Psychological Science* 14.2:273–291.

Druckman, James, Samara Klar, Yanna Krupnikov, Matthew Levendusky, and John Barry Ryan, 2022. "(Mis)estimating Affective Polarization." *The Journal of Politics* 84.2: 1106–1117.

Druckman, James, and Matthew Levendusky. 2019. "What Do We Measure Qhen We Measure Affective Polarization?" *Public Opinion Quarterly* 8.1: 114–122.

Economist Intelligence Unit (EIU). 2021. *Democracy Index*. https://www.eiu.com/n/campaigns/democracy-index-2021/.

Edsell, Thomas. 2019. "No Hate Left Behind." *The New York Times*, March 13.

Edsell, Thomas. 2021. "How to Tell When Your Country Is Past the Point of No Return." *New York Times*, December 15.

Elliott, Kevin. 2023. *Democracy for Busy People*. Chicago: University of Chicago Press.

Enos, Ryan D. 2017. *The Space Between Us*. Cambridge: Cambridge University Press.

Fiorina, Morris, and Samuel Abrams. 2008. "Polarization in the American Public: Misconceptions and Misreadings." *The Journal of Politics* 70.2: 556–560.

Fiorina, Morris, Samuel Abrams, and Jeremy Pope. 2005. *Culture War? The Myth of a Polarized America*. New York: Pearson Longman.

Fishkin, James S. 2018. *Democracy When the People Are Thinking*. New York: Oxford University Press.

Freiman, Christopher. 2020. *Why It's OK to Ignore Politics*. New York: Routledge.

Gaertner, Samuel, John Dovidio, Phyllis Anastasio, Betty Bachman, and Mary Rust. 1993. "The Common Ingroup Identity Model: Recategorization and the Reduction of Intergroup Bias." *European Review of Social Psychology* 4.1:1–26.

Gerber, Alan S., and Gregory A. Huber. 2009. "Partisanship and Economic Behavior: Do Partisan Differences in Economic Forecasts Predict Real Economic Behavior?" *American Political Science Review* 103.3: 407–426.

Green, Jeffrey. 2015. "Solace for the Frustrations of Silent Citizenship." *Citizenship Studies* 19.5: 492–506.

Groenendyk, Eric W., and Antonie J. Banks. 2014. "Emotional Rescue: How Affect Helps Partisans Overcome Collective Action Problems." *Political Psychology* 35.3: 359–378.

Guerrero, Alexander. 2014. "Against Elections: The Lottocratic Alternative." *Philosophy and Public Affairs* 42: 135–178.

Hannon, Michael. 2021. "Disagreement or Badmouthing? The Role of Expressive Discourse in Politics." In Elizabeth Edenberg and Michael Hannon, eds. *Political Epistemology*, 297–318. New York: Oxford University Press.

Hannon, Michael. 2022. "Are Knowledgeable Voters Better Voters?" *Politics, Philosophy, and Economics* 21.1: 29–54.

Harvard Youth Poll. 2023. https://iop.harvard.edu/youth-poll/45th-edition-spring-2023.

Hastie, Reid, David Schkade, and Cass R. Sunstein. 2007. "What Happened on Deliberation Day?" *California Law Review* 95: 915–940.

Hetherington, Marc, Meri T. Long, and Thomas J. Rudolph. 2016. "Revisiting the Myth: New Evidence of a Polarized America." *Public Opinion Quarterly* 80.1: 321–350.

Hetherington, Marc, and Jonathan Weiler. 2018. *Prius or Pickup?* Boston: Houghton Mifflin Harcourt.

Hitz, Zena. 2020. *Lost In Thought*. Princeton: Princeton University Press.

Hogg, Michael A. 2001. "A Social Identity Theory of Leadership." *Personality and Social Psychology Review* 5: 184–200.

Huber, Gregory A., and Neil Malhotra. 2017. "Political Homophily in Social Relationships: Evidence from Online Dating Behavior." *The Journal of Politics* 79: 269–283.

Hudson, Alexandra. 2023. *The Soul of Civility*. New York: St. Martin's Press.

International IDEA. 2021. *Global State of Democracy Report*. https://www.idea.int/gsod-2021/.

International IDEA. 2022. *Global State of Democracy Report*. https://www.idea.int/democracytracker/gsod-report-2022.
International IDEA. 2023. *Global State of Democracy Report*. https://www.idea.int/publications/catalogue/global-state-democracy-2023-new-checks-and-balances.
Iyengar, Shanto, and Tobias Konitzer. 2017. "The Moderating Effects of Marriage across Party Lines." Working paper. https://pdfs.semanticscholar.org/a55b/50f3de44529ee301c662aa42fb244e4ab992.pdf.
Iyengar, Shanto, Tobias Konitzer, and Kent Tedin. 2018. "The Home as a Political Fortress: Family Agreement in an Era of Polarization." *The Journal of Politics* 80.4: 1326–1338.
Iyengar, Shanto, and Masha Krupenkin. 2018. "The Strengthening of Partisan Affect." *Advances in Political Psychology* 39: 201–218.
Iyengar, Shanto, Yphtach Lelkes, Matthew Levendusky, Neil Malhotra, and Sean J. Westwood. 2019. "The Origins and Consequences of Affective Polarization in the United States." *Annual Review of Political Science* 22: 129–146.
Iyengar, Shanto, Guarav Sood, and Yphach Lelkes. 2012. "Affect, not Ideology: A Social Identity Perspective on Polarization." *Public Opinion Quarterly* 76: 405–431.
Iyengar, Shanto, and Sean J. Westwood. 2015. "Fear and Loathing Across Party Lines: New Evidence on Group Polarization." *American Journal of Political Science* 59: 690–707.
Jenke, Libby. 2023. "Affective Polarization and Misinformation Belief." *Political Behavior* 18: 1–60.
Joshi, Hrishilkesh. 2020. "What Are the Chances You're Right about Everything? An Epistemic Challenge to Modern Partisanship." *Politics, Philosophy, and Economics* 19.1: 36–61.
Jost, J. T., Sander van der Linden, Costas Panagopoulos, and Curtis D. Hardin. 2018. "Ideological Asymmetries in Conformity, Desire for Shared Reality, and the Spread of Misinformation." *Current Opinion in Psychology* 23: 77–83.
Kalmoe, Nathan, and Lilliana Mason. 2019. "Lethal Mass Partisanship." Working paper. https://www.dannyhayes.org/uploads/6/9/8/5/69858539/kalmoe___mason_ncapsa_2019_-_lethal_partisanship_-_final_lmedit.pdf.
Kalmoe, Nathan, and Lilliana Mason. 2022. *Radical American Partisanship*. Chicago: University of Chicago Press.
Kaplan, Ethan, Jorg Spenkuch, and Rebecca Sullivan. 2022. "Partisan Spatial Sorting in the United States: A Theoretical and Empirical Overview." *Journal of Public Economics* 211: n.p.
Keith, William, and Robert Danisch. 2020. *Beyond Civility*. University Park: Pennsylvania State University Press.

Klein, Ezra. 2020. *Why We're Polarized*. New York: Avid Reader Press.

Klofstad, Casey A., Rose McDermott, and Peter K. Hatemi. 2013. "The Dating Preference of Liberals and Conservatives." *Political Behavior* 35.3: 519–538.

Kolbert, Elizabeth. 2022. "How Politics Got So Polarized." *The New Yorker*, January 3.

Kolodny, Niko. 2023. *The Pecking Order*. Cambridge, MA: Harvard University Press.

Lafont, Cristina. 2020. *Democracy Without Shortcuts*. New York: Oxford University Press.

Lamm, Helmut, and David Myers. 1978. "Group-Induced Polarization of Attitudes and Behavior." *Advances in Experimental Social Psychology* 11: 145–187.

Landemore, Hélène. 2012. *Democratic Reason*. Princeton, NJ: Princeton University Press.

Landemore, Hélène. 2020. *Open Democracy: Reinventing Popular Rule for the Twenty-First Century*. Princeton, NJ: Princeton University Press.

Layman, Geoffrey C., and Thomas M. Carsey. 2002. "Party Polarization and 'Conflict Extension' in the American Electorate." *American Journal of Political Science* 46.4: 786–802.

Lee, Amber Hye-Yon. 2021. "How the Politicization of Everyday Activities Affects the Public Sphere: The Effects of Partisan Stereotypes on Cross-Cutting Interactions." *Political Communication* 38.5: 499–518.

Lee, E. J. 2007. "Deindividuation Effects on Group Polarization in Computer-Mediated Communication: The Role of Group Identification, Public-Self-Awareness, and Perceived Argument Quality." *Journal of Communication* 57: 385–403.

Lee, Frances E. 2016. *Insecure Majorities: Congress and the Perpetual Campaign*. Chicago: University of Chicago Press.

Levendusky, Matthew. 2009. *The Partisan Sort*. Chicago: University of Chicago Press.

Levendusky, Matthew, and Neil Malhorta. 2016. "Does Media Coverage of Partisan Polarization Affect Politics Attitudes?" *Political Commun* 33: 283–301.

López-Guerra, Claudio. 2011. "The Enfranchisement Lottery." *Philosophy, Politics, and Economics* 10: 211–233.

MacIntyre, Alasdair. 1981. *After Virtue*. Notre Dame, IN: University of Notre Dame Press.

Margolis, Michele F. 2018. *From Politics to the Pews*. Chicago: University of Chicago Press.

Margolis, Michele F., and Michael Sances. 2017. "Partisan Differences in Nonpartisan Activity: The Case of Charitable Giving." *Political Behavior* 39: 839–864.

Marques, José M., Vincent Y. Yzerbyt, and Jacques-Philippe Leyens. 1988. "The 'Black Sheep Effect': Extremity of Judgments towards Ingroup Members as a Function of Group Identification." *European Journal of Social Psychology* 18: 1–16.

Martin, Danielle, and Alessandro Nai. 2024. "Deepening the Rift: Negative Campaigning Fosters Affective Polarization in Multiparty Elections." *Electoral Studies* online first.

Mason, Lilliana. 2015. "'I Disrespectfully Agree': The Differential Effects of Partisan Sorting on Social and Issue Polarization." *American Journal of Political Science* 59: 128–145.

Mason, Lilliana. 2018a. *Uncivil Agreement: How Politics Became our Identity.* Chicago: University of Chicago Press.

Mason, Lilliana. 2018b. "Ideologues without Issues: The Polarizing Consequences of Ideological Identities." *Public Opinion Quarterly* 82: 280–301.

Mason, Lilliana, and Julie Wronski. 2018. "One Tribe to Bind Them All: How Our Social Group Attachments Strengthen Partisanship." *Political Psychology* 39: 257–277.

McConnell, Christopher, Yotam Margalit, Neil Malhotra, and Matthew Levendusky. 2017. "The Economic Consequences of Partisanship in a Polarized Era." *American Journal of Political Science* 62: 5–18.

Mendelberg, Tali. 2002. "The Deliberative Citizen: Theory and Evidence." In Michael X. Delli Carpini, Leonie Huddy, and Robert Y. Shapiro, eds. *Research in Micropolitics*, vol. 6: *Political Decision Making, Deliberation, and Participation.* Amsterdam: Elsevier.

Monmouth University Poll. 2023. "Partisan Identity Determines which Specific Rights People Feel Are at Risk." https://www.monmouth.edu/polling-/reports/monmouthpoll_US_062023/.

Moore-Berg, Samantha L., Boaz Hameiri, and Emile Bruneau. 2020. "The Prime Psychological Suspects of Toxic Political Polarization." *Current Opinion in Behavioral Sciences* 34: 199–204.

More In Common. 2019. "The Perception Gap." https://perceptiongap.us/.

Moscovici, S., and M. Zavalloni. 1969. "The Group as a Polarizer of Attitudes." *Journal of Personality and Social Psychology* 12: 125–135.

Mutz, Diana. 2006. *Hearing the Other Side: Deliberative versus Participatory Democracy.* Cambridge: Cambridge University Press.

Mutz, Diana. 2013. "Reflections on Hearing the Other Side, in Theory and in Practice." *Critical Review* 25.2: 260–276.

Mutz, Diana, and Jeffrey Mondak. 2006. "The Workplace as a Context for Cross-Cutting Political Discourse." *The Journal of Politics* 68.1: 140–155.

Myers, D. G. 1975. "Discussion-Induced Attitude Polarization." *Human Relations* 28: 699–714.

Myers, D. G., and G. D. Bishop. 1970. "Discussion Effects on Racial Attitudes." *Science* 169.3947: 778–779.

Myers, D. G., J. B. Bruggink, R. C. Kersting, and B. A. Schlosser. 1980. "Does Learning Others' Opinions Change One's Opinion?" *Personality and Social Psychology Bulletin* 6: 253–260.

Neblo, Michael, Kevin M. Esterling, Ryan P. Kennedy, David M. J. Lazer, and Anana E. Sokhey. 2010. "Who Wants to Deliberate—and Why?" *American Political Science Review* 104: 566–583.

Nicholson, Stephen, Chelsea M. Coe, Jason Emory, and Anna V. Song 2016. "The Politics of Beauty: The Effects of Partisan Bias on Physical Attractiveness." *Political Behavior* 38.4: 883–898.

Nyhan, Brendan. 2020. "Facts and Myths about Misperceptions." *Journal of Economic Perspectives* 34.3: 220–236.

Nyhan, Brendan, and Jason Reifler. 2010. "When Corrections Fail: The Persistence of Political Misperceptions." *Political Behavior* 32: 303–330.

Parkinson, John. 2012. *Democracy and Public Space*. New York: Oxford University Press.

Peet, Lisa. 2022. "Uncertain Times: Budgets and Funding 2022." *Library Journal*, February 1.

Pettit, Philip. 2012. *On the People's Terms*. Cambridge: Cambridge University Press.

Pew Research Center. 2014. "Political Polarization in the American Public." https://www.pewresearch.org/politics/2014/06/12/political-polarization-in-the-american-public/.

Pew Research Center. 2019a. "Americans Say the Nation's Political Debate has Grown More Toxic and 'Heated' Rhetoric Could Lead to Violence." https://www.pewresearch.org/short-reads/2019/07/18/americans-say-the-nations-political-debate-has-grown-more-toxic-and-heated-rhetoric-could-lead-to-violence/.

Pew Research Center. 2019b. "Partisans Say Respect and Compromise are Important in Politics—Particularly from Their Opponents." https://www.pewresearch.org/fact-tank/2019/06/19/partisans-say-respect-and-compromise-are-important-in-politics-particularly-from-their-opponents/.

Pew Research Center. 2021. "Republicans and Democrats Alike Say it's Stressful to Talk about Politics with People who Disagree." https://www.pewresearch.org/short-reads/2021/11/23/republicans-and-democrats-alike-say-its-stressful-to-talk-politics-with-people-who-disagree/.

Pew Research Center. 2023. "Inflation, Health Costs, Partisan Cooperation Among the Nation's Top Problems." https://www.pewresearch.org/politics/2023/06/21/inflation-health-costs-partisan-cooperation-among-the-nations-top-problems/.

Puglisi, Riccardo, and James M. Snyder. 2011. "Newspaper Coverage of Political Scandals." *Journal of Politics* 73: 931–950.

Putnam, Robert D. 1995. "Bowling Alone: America's Declining Social Capital." *Journal of Democracy* 6.1: 65–78.

Rawlings, Craig M., and Clayton Childress. 2023. "The Polarization of Popular Culture." *Social Forces* online first.

Rawls, John. 2005. *Political Liberalism*. Expanded edition. New York: Columbia University Press.
Rose, Julie. 2016. *Free Time*. Princeton, NJ: Princeton University Press.
Saad, Lydia. 2023. "Historically Low Faith in U. S. Institutions Continues." https://news.gallup.com/poll/508169/historically-low-faith-institutions-continues.aspx.
Saguy, T., and Eran Halperin. 2014. "Exposure to Outgroup Members Criticizing their Own Group Facilitates Intergroup Openness." *Personality and Social Psychology Bulletin* 40.6: 791–802.
Sandel, Michael. 1982. *Liberalism and the Limits of Justice*. Cambridge: Cambridge University Press.
Santoro, Erik and David E. Brockman. 2022. "The Primise and Pitfalls of Cross-partisan Conversations for Reducing Affective Polarization: Evidence from Randomized Experiments." *Science Advances* 8.25: 1–16.
Shafranek, Richard. 2020. "Political Consequences of Partisan Prejudice." *Political Psychology* 41.1: 35–51.
Shepard, Steven. 2023. "The Data's Clear: The Indictment Makes Republicans Like Trump More." https://www.politico.com/news/2023/03/31/donald-trump-indictment-00090001.
Simmons, A. John. 1980. *Moral Principles and Political Obligations*. Princeton, NJ: Princeton University Press.
Somin, Ilya. 2013. *Democracy and Public Ignorance*. Stanford, CA: Stanford University Press.
Sood, Guarav, and Shanto Iyengar. 2016. "Coming to Dislike your Opponents: The Polarizing Impact of Political Campaigns." Working paper: https://www.gsood.com/research/papers/ComingToDislike.pdf. Accessed October 7, 2020.
Stoker, Laura, and M. Kent Jennings. 1995. "The Home as a Political Fortress: Family Agreement in an Era of Polarization." *American Political Science Review* 89.2: 421–433.
Stoner, James. 1968. "Risky and Cautious Shifts in Group Decisions: The Influence of Widely Held Values." *Journal of Experimental Social Psychology* 4.4: 442–459.
Sunstein, Cass R. 2009. *Going to Extremes: How Like Minds Unite and Divide*. New York: Oxford University Press.
Sunstein, Cass R. 2017. *#Republic*. Princeton, NJ: Princeton University Press.
Sunstein, Cass. 2019. *Conformity*. New York: New York University Press.
Taber, Charles, and Milton Lodge. 2006. "Motivated Skepticism in the Evaluation of Political Beliefs." *American Journal of Political Science* 50.3: 755–769.
Talisse, Robert B. 2019. *Overdoing Democracy: Why We Must Put Politics in its Place*. New York: Oxford University Press.

Talisse, Robert B. 2021. *Sustaining Democracy: What We Owe to the Other Side.* New York: Oxford University Press.

Tam Cho, Wendy K., James G. Gimpel, and Iris S. Hui. 2013. "Voter Migration and the Geographic Sorting of the American Electorate." *Annals of the Association of American Geographers* 103: 856–870.

Thomsen, Jens Peter, and Anna H. Thomsen. 2022. "Intergroup Contact Reduces Affective Polarization but not Among Strong Party Identifiers." *Scandinavian Political Studies* 46: 241–263.

Turner, John C., Michael A. Hogg, Penelope J. Oakes, Stephen D. Reicher, and Margaret S. Wetherell. 1987. *Rediscovering the Social Group: A Self-Categorization Theory.* New York: Basil Blackwell.

US Surgeon General. 2023. "Our Epidemic of Loneliness and Isolation." https://www.hhs.gov/sites/default/files/surgeon-general-social-connection-advisory.pdf.

Vaidhyanathan, Siva. 2018. *Antisocial Media.* New York: Oxford University Press.

Valentino, Nicholas A., Ted Brader, Eric W. Groenendyk, Krysha Gregorowicz, and Vincent L. Hutchings. 2011. "Election Night's Alright for Fighting: The Role of Emotions in Political Participation." *The Journal of Politics* 73.1: 156–170.

Van Bavel, Jay J., Steve Rathje, Madalina Vlasceanu, and Clara Pretus. 2024. "Updating the Identity-Based Model of Belief: From False Belief to Misinformation." *Current Opinion in Psychology* 56: Article 101787.

Van Swol, Lyn M. 2009. "Extreme Members and Group Polarization." *Social Influence* 4.3: 185–199.

Voelkel, Jan G., James Chu, Michael N. Stagnaro, Joseph S. Mernyk, Chrystal Redekopp, Sophia L. Pink, James N. Druckman, David G. Rand, and Robb Willer. 2023. "Interventions Reducing Affective Polarization do not Necessarily Improve Anti-democratic Attitudes." *Nature Human Behaviour* 7: 55–64.

Wagner, Markus. 2021. "Affective Polarization in Multiparty Systems." *Electoral Studies* 69: 34–44.

Waldron, Jeremy. 2017. *One Another's Equals.* Cambridge, MA: Harvard University Press.

Wang, Chris, Michael J. Platow, and Eryn J. Newman. 2023. "There Is an 'I' in Truth: How Salient Identities Shape Dynamic Perceptions of Truth." *European Journal of Social Psychology* 53.2: 383–400.

West, Emily A., and Shanto Iyengar. 2020. "Partisanship as a Social Identity: Implications for Polarization." *Political Behavior* 44: 807–838.

Westfall, Jacob, Leaf Van Boven, John R. Chambers, and Charles M. Judd. 2015. "Perceiving Political Polarization in the United States: Party Identity Strength and Attitude Extremity Exacerbate the Perceived Partisan Divide." *Perspectives on Psychological Science* 10: 145–158.

Westwood, Sean J., Shanto Iyengar, Stefaan Walgrave, Rafael Leonisio, Luis Miller, and Oliver Strijbis. 2017. "The Tie that Divides: Cross-national Evidence of the Primacy of Partyism." *European Journal of Political Research* 57.2: 333–335.

Williams, Bernard. 1973. "A Critique of Utilitarianism." In J. J. C. Smart and Bernard Williams, eds. *Utilitarianism: For and Against*, 75–150. Cambridge: Cambridge University Press.

Wojcieszak, Magdalena, and Benjamin Warner. 2020. "Can Interparty Contact Reduce Affective Polarization? A Systematic Test of Different Forms of Intergroup Contact." *Political Communication* 37.6: 789–811.

Wolff, Robert P. 1970. *In Defense of Anarchism*. New York: Harper.

Zamalin, Alex. 2021. *Against Civility*. New York: Beacon Press.

Index

For the benefit of digital users, indexed terms that span two pages (e.g., 52–53) may, on occasion, appear on only one of those pages.

2020 Presidential Election, xi–xii, 65

Addams, Jane, ix
advocates versus advertisers, 127–28
airline pilots, 113–14, 128–29
"alternate reality," 112–13
anarchism, 39, 45–46
animosity, 7–8, 22, 75–76, 95–96, 116, 121, 125–26
    localized, 73–74
    personalized, 73–74
antihierarchy, 41–42
apathy, 4
aristocracy, 40
Aristotle, 60–61, 118–19, 122, 139–45
Artificial Intelligence, 101
atopia, 139, 141–45, 152–53
Austen, Jane, 144

Bach, 61
belief polarization, 7–8, 26, 70, 77–87, 93–94
    centering group identity, 87
    Comparison View of, 82–83
    content of beliefs, 79
    Corroboration View of, 83–84, 86–87, 89, 94, 135–36
    degree of belief, 79
    Information View of, 81–82
    not reason-responsive, 113
    related to affective polarization, 88–89, 94, 96–97

Biden, Joe, 65, 66
Bill of Rights, 43–44
Black Sheep Effect, 80–81
Braver Angels, 119–20
Bush, George W, 66

Callas, Maria, 61
Carter, Jimmy, 66
causation, 13
character traits, 117–18
citizens, 1
citizenship, 19, 20–21, 29, 33–34, 152
    as conflicted, 68–69
    ethics of, viii–ix, 16
    involves a civic ethos, 35
    as a moral office, 20–21, 46
    as public and collective, 3
civic responsibilities, 20–21, 46, 47
civic solitude, 2–3, 23–24, 27, 107–8, 135, 145, 158–59
    places to engage in, 146–47
civil hygiene, 128–29
Civil Rights, 43–44, 59–60, 156
civility, 14, 22, 54–59, 64, 68, 114–16, 122
    as internally conflicted, 64, 103
    opportunity to model, 123
    as reciprocal, 58
    as recognition, 54–56
    as undermined by polarization dynamic, 99–100, 101
climate change, 101
clique, 87
common good, 48–50, 54, 110–11

Communitarianism, 164n.8
competence, 32–33, 48, 110
complacency, 2
confidence, 78–79, 126–27, 130–31
conformity, 7–8, 22, 23–24, 81, 97–98
Congress, 65
conservative, 18–19, 141–42
   partisan sorting in United States, 90–91
   political saturation in United States, 92–93
   "Was Aristotle a…?" 139–41
Conservative Party
   in Panopolis, 154
conspiracy theories, 24
constitution, 37, 156
contemplation, 8, 150
contempt, 75
contestation, 44–46, 50, 133
   as reason-governed, 51
   versus complaining, 50–51, 111
Coors beer, 91
corporations, 86
corruption, 11
counterfeit democracy, 30–31
COVID-19 Pandemic, 97
cowardice, 118
Cracker Barrell, 91
cults, 24, 112–13
Curative Fallacy, 13–15, 23–24, 107, 123

De Gaulle, Charles, 77
democracy
   as aspiration, 6, 62, 99–100, 108, 128, 131, 159
   having internal dysfunction, 4
   ideal, 37–38, 59
   as an institution, 35
   representative, 1
   as self-governing society of equals, 37–38, 59, 63–64, 159
   skepticism about, 4, 32, 33
   as social ideal, 37–38, 59, 159
   subject to autoimmune disorder, viii–ix, 69, 103–5, 106, 152
   tragic, 151
Democracy Index, 65–66
democracy versus republic, 16–18
Democratic Party, 18, 73
   symmetrical affective polarization, 166n.24
Denver, Colorado, 78
depolarization, 121
descriptive, 9
Devil's Advocacy, 132
Dewey-Addams Principle, ix
Dewey, John, ix, x, 108
disagreement, 39, 40, 56, 67, 127, 143
dispositions, 34
distance, 23–24, 147, 158–59
   conceptual, 137–38
   social, 135–36, 145
   social versus conceptual, 107–8
   spatial, 145–46
dogmatism, 78–79
Dunkin Donuts, 91
Dylan, Bob, 61

Earth, 59, 60
echo chambers, 26
Election Day, 150–51, 152
elections, 35, 36–37, 45, 50, 59–60, 142, 156
elitism, 148–50
equality, 38–40, 44–45, 128, 151
   live together as equals, 38
   and political difference, 55
   political equals, 8, 20–21, 45–46
   recognize one another as equals, 49, 50, 58, 104, 111
equal standing, 41, 44, 46, 52
   as a relation, 42

facilitated democracy, 116–24
fake news, 112–13

fallibilism, 133
fascism, 149–50
free time, 149
free-riding, 47–48
freedom, 156

generosity, 118
Georgia, 91
Global State of Democracy, 65–66
Google search
   for "democracy," 35, 45
   for "This is what democracy looks like," 1, 6, 29, 34–35, 45, 109, 160
Gould, Glenn, 61
group polarization, 167n.46

hardliners, 72
hierarchy, 81, 140–41
homophily, 92
Humanities, 25, 144–45

ignorance, 31, 32–33
imagination, 8, 57, 102, 138, 143–44, 159–60
immigration, 31
incivility, 14, 15, 58
intergenerational duties, 46–47
International IDEA, 65–66
internet, 26

justice, 21, 48–49, 54, 159

legitimacy, 21
leisure, 2
liberal education, 25
Liberal Party
   in Panopolis, 154
liberals, 18–19, 141–42
   partisan sorting in United States, 90–91
   political saturation in United States, 92–93

liberty, 44, 149–50
libraries, 24–26, 146–48
likeminded groups, 77, 78, 80
Lincoln Memorial Reflecting Pool, 160–61
literal, 84
loneliness, 5
lottery, 142
luxury, 2

majority rule, 17, 43
mass incarceration, 11, 101
Mencius, 143–44
misinformation, 97, 101
mitigation, ix–x, 10
mobilization, 156, 157
Montgomery, Wes, 61
Mozart, 61
MSNBC, 93–94
museums, 24–26, 146–48, 160–61

national identity, 149–50
National Mall, 160–61
"neoliberal," 165n.19
Newton, Isaac, 60
Nicomachean Ethics, 117–18
normative, 9–10, 12

Overdoing Democracy, vii, ix–x, 5

Panopolis, 154–57
parks, 25–26, 146–48, 160–61
parties, 7
partisan identity, 88–89
   as centered, 22–24, 69, 90, 92, 122–23, 131, 137, 145–46
   decentering, 124–25, 130–34, 137–38, 152–53
   involving sorting and saturation of social space, 23
   as lifestyle, 23, 91–92
partisan saturation, 92–94, 123, 132–33, 145, 156–57

partisan society, 155
partisan sorting, 90–92, 123, 132–33, 154–55
Parton, Dolly, 61
patriotic duties, 46–47
patriotism, 155
perception gap, 74–75, 97
personal approach to polarization management, 125–30, 131–32, 143
perspective taking. *see* imagination
Plato, 144
polarization, 28, 68, 112, 120–22, 126
　as a management task, 106, 121–22, 143
　in popular use, 65–66
　as stealthy, 113, 115, 158
polarization dynamic, 7, 9–11, 22–24, 69, 95–103, 112, 137
　in Panopolis, 157
political polarization, 65–66, 70, 87–88
　affective polarization, site of, 72–75, 87–89, 94, 96–97, 166n.42
　elite polarization, site of, 71–72
　platform polarization, site of, 71, 76
　three sites as mutually reinforcing, 75–76
political rallies, 86
politics vs. political theory, 16
poverty, 101
power, 39, 43, 44, 45–46, 110, 149–50
Press, 7, 50, 59–60
preventing versus reversing, 13
privacy, 2
projects, 62
propaganda, 30–31
public reasons, 51
public space, 29
public-mindedness, 47–50, 52, 53

racism, 101
radicalization, 135

reasons, 113
　reason-responsive, 138
recognition, 42
reconciliation, 129–30, 131
recourse, 44
reflection, 3, 5, 7, 8, 24–25, 107–8
　atopic political, 143–44
　capacities for, 8
　and citizenship, 64, 104, 110
　distanced, 23–24, 107–8, 135, 137
　and political action, 20–21
　settings for, 146
　in solitude, 135
　undermined by democratic action, 104
relational approach to polarization management, 116–24, 125–26, 129–30
remedial democratic theory, 10, 15, 20
Republican Party, 65, 73
　symmetrical affective polarization, 166n.24
respite, 5
responsiveness, 47, 49–50, 52–53
"RINO," 165n.19
rock concerts, 86

self-criticism, 134–35, 137, 139, 152–53, 169n.17
self-monitoring, 114
self-regulation, 126, 160
snobbery, 61
social disadvantage, 147–48, 151–52
social holism, 40
socialism, 149–50
spatial detachment. *see* distance
sports fans, 85–86
"start small" approach, 28, 160
subordination, 40, 43–45, 111, 159
Supreme Court, 65
Sustaining Democracy, vii, viii, ix–x
Swift, Taylor, 61

terrorism, 101
transparency, 47, 52–53
Trump, Donald, 65

uncivil, the, 57–59
　merely uncivil, the, 58
United States, xi, 10–11
　affective polarization in, 72, 73
　conservative and liberal partisan affiliation in, 23, 90–95
　as a democracy or republic, 16–17
　elite polarization in, 72
　polarization in, 65–66

United States Constitution, 16–17, 18
uptake, 50–51
utopia, 9

virtues and vices, 117–18, 139–40
voting, 1–2, 35, 75–76, 98, 110, 151

Walker, David, 143–44
Walmart, 93–94
Washington, DC, 160
White House, 65
Whole Foods, 93–94
Wollstonecraft, Mary, 143–44